WELCOME HOME

RICHARD CACIOPPE

Welcome Home

Richard Cacioppe

ISBN (Print Edition): 978-1-54396-434-9

ISBN (eBook Edition): 978-1-54396-435-6

Forsan et haec olim meminisse iuvabit (Perhaps there shall come a day when it will be sweet to remember even these things.) Virgil, Aeneid, Book 1, line 203 Quoted by Victor Davis Hanson in Ripples of Battle

FOREWORD

War leaves little of value in its wake. Foremost among its meager gifts is the bond of friendship between men, forged in adversity and tempered by the loss and sting of battle. It is ironic that the worst of man's endeavors should yield one of humanity's purest products.

Friendship among women has long been discussed and celebrated. However, there is almost no mention of the importance of friendship among men, especially those who become united during difficult times. The silence about these relationships is intentional. Men in these friendships communicate at a different level, an almost primeval level which requires very little spoken communication. These men are careful to mask their feelings so that even those in their presence are unable to see the signs of friendship that are exchanged. A brief hug or a slap on the back conveys enormous messages to other members of the brotherhood. They care not to understand their own emotions nor dare to plumb the depths of the love they feel for one another. They're content to know that it is.

These stories of unspoken affection and uncommon friendship swirl unseen around you every day. The stories of these friendships are known only to the men who live them and barely understood even by them. This is one of those stories.

This book is dedicated to the more than 2 1/2 million men and women who served in Vietnam. They answered their country's call to fight in an unpopular war under very difficult conditions. Many of them returned home not to a grateful nation but instead to the hostility of their fellow citizens. For those that waited for us, we say thank you. For those who asked why we went, we say "You sent us, I thought you knew."

There is a custom today among Vietnam vets, almost unknown to those who were not there. These old soldiers long ago put aside the rejection they felt when they came home. Because there were no celebrations when they returned, VN vets celebrate the brotherhood of those with whom they served by simply and quietly saying to one another 'Welcome Home' when they meet.

1967
WELCOME HOME

The huge C-141 circled gracefully over the New Jersey countryside, then glided in a lazy descent to the airfield below. The soft touchdown of the huge craft was barely perceptible to its occupants. The plane slowly meandered along the access routes of the airport to its designated unloading point before coming to a stop. As if giving one final yawn to signify the end of its long journey, the rear ramp of the aircraft opened slowly.

Almost immediately, the soldiers on board hurried off, anxious to be on the ground after the long flight. Without direction, they placed their duffel bags in a pile and gathered in a loose military formation. Their nervous energy was very apparent as they hugged one another, unashamed of showing their joy at finally coming home. To the amusement of their companions, several of the soldiers kneeled down and kissed the tarmac. The bright spring morning provided a perfect backdrop to the joyous gathering on the runway. Off in the distance, the men could see a convoy of blue Air Force busses making their way, single file, toward them. When the lead bus stopped in front of the group, an army captain with a clipboard got off. The men instinctively got into a tighter, more military formation when they saw him. They quieted down so they could hear the officer's instructions.

The captain's instructions were brief, detailing the events which would take place before the men would be released to go home. He then pointed to a distant point at the edge of the base where the troops could barely see that a crowd had gathered. The officer sadly apologized as he explained that the crowd had assembled to protest their opposition to the war. He then read from a prepared statement explaining the crowd's right to gather and gave instructions to the soldiers not to become involved or interfere with the crowd as the busses passed through the area.

The mood of the gathered soldiers changed perceptibly as they listened to the officer. They focused now on the crowd which they had barely noticed previously. Their earlier ebullient enthusiasm and confidence seemed to be replaced by an air of confusion and uncertainty.

When he finished, the captain directed the men to load the busses. They gathered up their duffel bags and quickly got onto the buses, still warily watching the crowd in the distance.

While some of the soldiers stoically ignored the protesters, the majority of the men watched through the windows as the vehicles approached the crowd. The busses paused at the entrance to the gate as the military policemen pushed into the crowd to provide clearance for the double gate to open.

As the vehicles made their way slowly past the crowd, they were pelted by tomatoes, eggs and rotten fruit. The contrast between the silence in the bus and the screaming and other noises of the crowd was striking. The impassive and disbelieving faces of the soldiers were also in contrast to the emotional, contorted and ugly faces of the demonstrators.

As the last bus slowly pulled away from the crowd, a single soldier made his way to the rear to catch a final glimpse of the chaotic scene. He watched the crowd recede into the distance as the bus picked up speed and he muttered to himself over and over again, "Oh my God."

CHAPTER ONE

1992
HENRY

Marco sped up the long, curving driveway. No matter how early he awakened in the morning, it seemed he was always fifteen minutes late. The 8 o'clock morning news was just concluding, which meant he was already five minutes late.

As he careened around the last turn into the employee parking lot, all of his folders and papers slid off the back seat and fell to the floor in a jumbled mess. As usual, the parking lot was almost filled, so Marco had to drive to the farthest point to park his battered Volkswagen.

He jumped out of the car and quickly scooped up the pile of papers from the car floor while his car continued to sputter and gasp before giving out in a last mournful wheeze." Run on", Tony had described it to him without hearing it. That reminded Marco that Tony had made another appointment for the car that afternoon. Since he already had missed two, Marco knew he better not cancel a third time.

He stuffed the papers and folders under his arm and raced for the door. He quickly opened it and sprinted down the hallway, attempting at the same time to mold his pile of papers into a compact bundle. He slowed to a walk when he got close to the computer room, trying at the same time to control his breathing so his entrance would be as inconspicuous as possible. Having gotten this far undetected, he felt elated. He chuckled to himself as he remembered those old movies where Dagwood raced out of his house every morning and collided with the mailman on his front lawn." At least I haven't done that," he mumbled to himself then chuckled again when he realized that Dagwood probably wasn't a good role model for many people.

He pretended he hadn't heard his name and continued to walk slowly and deliberately to his cubicle clenching his teeth tightly in an attempt to regain his breath without gasping." Covello," the voice had followed him to his desk.

"Yes Henry," the words almost exploded out of Marco's mouth when he couldn't hold his breath any longer.

"Nice of you to join us this morning, Covello. This is the fourth time this week that you've been late. Are you trying for some kind of world record? What did you do in Vietnam, tell the Vietcong to wait until you arrived each morning?"

Marco stiffened and glared at his boss, and quickly looked away and began straightening the papers on his desk. The older man, aware now that he had captured the attention of the whole office, moved belligerently closer, thrusting his long, thin face closer to Marco's. Because of the closeness of the two, Marco was forced to look into Henry's eyes, thinking to himself how colorless they were. Henry's skinny and badly wrinkled neck was extended, exaggerating the poor fit of the shirt he wore. His Adam's apple moved up and down seemingly uncontrollably, as he groped for words to continue his tirade. Now that he had everyone's attention, he became increasingly agitated that he couldn't come up with anything clever to say. His mouth worked and his eyes bulged, yet no words came out. Marco, feeling almost embarrassed for Henry, looked away and started to straighten his papers again. The other workers, having been witness to this same series of events many times, now also lost interest.

Gradually, the hum of activity returned to the room. Only Henry seemed fixed, intent on preserving the moment until he could come up with a clever continuation of his reprimand.

"Fishgrund, I really admire you." Tony's jovial, booming voice drew everyone's attention back to the center of the room." Here you are, the corporate data processing manager, taking time to greet one of your employees while the entire corporation grinds to a halt because the system is down. What a guy! I have to tell everyone upstairs how calm you are."

Henry turned his head so swiftly it made a cracking sound. Unintelligible little sounds finally emerged from his mouth. "What do you mean?" His voice seemed almost unnaturally high-pitched.

"I don't know. I was in the computer room trying to get my salesmen's commission reports when someone said,'Head crash.' Everyone started running and shouting. Is a head crash bad, Henry?"

Henry gave out a low moan, which then changed to a whining sound while he started to rock from one foot to the other.

"What a guy! Calm as you please, taking time to talk to one of his troops while he's being overrun. He's the kind of guy we needed with us in the war, huh Marco?"

As Henry's head turned again, Marco who was grinning ear to ear, immediately resumed the serious look he had had before.

Henry looked from Marco to Tony, his head jerking from side to side, reminding Marco of a turtle, checking to see if it was safe to cross a road. After a few more whining sounds, Henry seemed to be jolted into action. He ran from the room, his shirt hanging over his belt flapping behind him. As soon as the door slammed behind Henry, the room exploded in laughter.

"Thanks for bringing the news and getting Henry off my case Tony. Your timing couldn't have been much better."

"That's okay pal, but you don't have much time before he gets back. By then, you'd better be deeply immersed in your work."

"Nah, you're wrong Tony, a head crash is serious. He'll be gone all day."

The smile spread on Tony's face."There was no head crashed," he said smugly."It's almost totally true. Well… I was a little deceptive. Actually, I stretched the truth considerably." Tony paused for dramatic effect as Marco's smiling face changed to one of puzzlement and concern."To be honest, I lied," Tony continued. A car crash isn't much different than a head crash is it Marco?"

The grin widened on Marco's face. "The big difference is that a good body man can fix a fender in a short time. It'll take all the kings horses and all the kings men to accumulate and reenter all the data that might be lost in the head crash."

"Well, thanks for today's computer lesson. How come you were late again today? You left before I did this morning."

"I went to get fresh buns from the bakery to take to my dad. You know the old man, he loves fresh baked goods from Angelo's. It makes his whole day. Once I got there, my mom had to fix me breakfast. She says I look too skinny. I blamed it on you. I told her that now that you're a big executive, you're trying to pass for American. I said you won't allow food in the house so that you can get skinny, emaciated and waspish."

"She knows me better than that, she loves me. She wouldn't believe that crap," Tony answered.

"You know what she said?" Marco continued," She gave me another one of those Italian pearls of wisdom. She said, 'Ne mange, ne binna Ga Ga.'"

"What does that mean?" Tony asked.

"Aa ha, I'm right you are trying to pass. You don't even know one of the key philosophical cornerstones of our heritage," Marco replied.

"Hey listen pal, I'm almost a pilgrim. I'm third generation American, how should I know what it means?"

"It means… if you don't eat, you don't shit." Both men laughed at Marco's translation.

"Somewhere in that quote is centuries of Italian wisdom, I just don't know what it is," joked Tony. In between laughing he blurted out" The Chinese have Confucius, the Greeks have Aristotle and we have Ne mangia, ne binna gaga."

The laughter of each man seemed to cause the other to laugh harder, until both were laughing uncontrollably. They were leaning over the desk with tears running down their faces, when Henry strode back into the room. He was followed by a tall, well-dressed man.

Marco stopped laughing and stiffened when he saw the two men enter the room. Tony, aware of the arrival of the two men, ignored their entrance. He continued chuckling, then slowly and deliberately wiped the tears from his eyes and turned to face the two men.

Henry paused, glaring at Marco and Tony. His companion gave him a nudge, causing him to stumble in the direction of the two now silent men. They both strode over to Marco and Tony. Marco's unsmiling countenance was a complete contrast to the amused look on Tony's face. Both men had a look of expectation. It was clear that Marco was anticipating something unpleasant while Tony appeared to be waiting eagerly for the coming encounter.

"There was no head crash DeJulio," Henry blurted out" one of these days, your weird sense of humor is going to get you into trouble."

The smirk on Tony's face spread to a full smile as Henry continued his attack. The pitch of his voice got so high that he now spoke in a barely perceptible squeal.

"For a manager in this company, you don't show much regard for other managers or setting a good example for the employees."

"Now now Henry, calm down," Tony said in a calm and almost condescending tone. Really there has been no harm done. Besides, as the DP manager it's a good idea for you to get into the computer room now and then. If I didn't do these things to you, you might never go into that room. Your employees tell me you haven't even seen the new disk drive which came in last month."

Henry's face reddened. He tried to talk then finally blurted out," Oh yeah." His stern expression changed to one of panic as he looked imploringly at his companion.

Barrington Howell stepped forward. His six foot two inch frame was perfectly encased in an expensive blue silk suit. His slightly graying hair was impeccably groomed and provided a striking contrast to his tanned face. The look of displeasure and disdain on his face was apparent as he spoke." I'll handle this Henry." The impatience and disgust he felt over Henry's handling of the incident were obvious both on his face and in his voice." DeJulio, one day your childish pranks are going to get you fired, then you'll have some real problems. That is unless pushcarts come back into vogue, then at least you might be able to have a successful career. That's the kind of marketing and selling you know. Why old man Foster thinks your brand of selling is of any value to us here is beyond me."

The smile on Tony's face widened." Thank you pilgrim Howell, for that stirring reminder of your expansive view that all citizens of the United States are created equal as long as they had a relative on the Mayflower."

In an instant, the look of amusement on Tony's face faded, replaced by one far more threatening. He stepped toward Howell and thrust his face into the taller man's. After a moment,Tony stepped back smiling broadly again." Well, enough of this idle discussion of our ancestry, entertaining and educational though it is. Time to get back to work."

The room which had hushed during the brief encounter, started to hum again with the sounds of office work. Tony still smiling, strode past Howell to seek out Henry who was almost hiding behind him. "Fishgrund as always, you set the fashion standard around here. That's one of those new clip on suits, isn't it? Oh wow, and look at those shoes. You don't see those homemade shoes much anymore."

As the older man turned red and attempted a response, Tony breezed by him. At the door to the office he turned and yelled to Marco," See you at lunch, pal."

Marco waved. He suddenly felt alone, even though the room was filled with other people.

"You'd do much better in this company if you kept away from him, Covello," sneered Howell. "Didn't they tell you that you didn't have to stay together once you got off the boat?" With that comment, Howell wheeled and left the room.

Henry stepped forward to confront Marco. He stared at Marco, hands on his hips, once again ineffectively trying to participate belatedly in the exchange which had already ended.

Marco sat down and began to work, leaving Henry standing alone. With a glare, Henry turned quickly and returned to his office. Marco took a deep breath and looked at the pile of papers on his desk. He was grateful that he had avoided another prolonged and uncomfortable episode with Henry. Thanks to Tony, the encounter had been mercifully brief, and as usual when Tony was involved, it was comical.

CHAPTER TWO

MARCO

Thank God for Tony. He seemed always to be around to extricate Marco from Henry's annoying critiques. Marco appreciated and admired Tony's ability to quickly defuse each situation with humor that seemed always to befuddle Henry.

Marco was finding it increasingly difficult to control his own anger after five years of Henry's incessant criticisms of all aspects of his work. He told Tony he could feel his Sicilian begin to rise from his feet and take over his whole body when Henry began his attacks.

Tony was always amused at Marco's description of the source of his anger. He had laughingly advised Marco to try to be more like an unemotional WASP when dealing with Henry. As silly as that sounded, Marco tried it and found that it worked. Not only did it help him to control his own emotions, his non-reaction seem to frustrate Henry. However, Marco knew that down deep his suppressed anger was something more than just a Sicilian trait. Not only did they not discuss the source of his anger, they rarely talked about their time together in Vietnam. Tony wasn't reluctant to reminisce about his tour of duty in that conflict. Marco had heard him discuss the war with many other veterans on several occasions. But, Marco knew that Tony was sensitive about discussing anything with him that might pick at the psychological wounds that Marco still carried. So, they both played a game. Marco pretended he had no open issues about his time in Vietnam, and Tony didn't get near any topics which might reveal the lie.

It was a gnawing knot in the pit of his stomach that seemed to spread throughout his body against his will. He had learned over the years that the only way to suppress this debilitating feeling was to force himself to focus entirely on some other activity. Physical exertion was the best remedy. When that was not possible, Marco forced himself to mentally concentrate on a problem. He had learned that programming problems were the most effective way that he could divert his thoughts. He could lose himself in the computer code so completely that he excluded everything around him. His concentration during those times was almost trance-like. Those around him knew better than to try to intrude upon him when he was in this almost hypnotic state. They learned to use his laser-like focus to their advantage. They gave Marco the toughest debugging tasks.

However, it was becoming increasingly difficult for Marco to keep the unwanted emotions at bay. He hated the feeling he got when he knew the beast was trying to escape the boundaries he had tried to set. His stomach turned as waves of anger coursed through his body. His temples throbbed as he tried to suppress the rage he could feel building in his soul. At those times he knew he had to be alone as he tried to recover control of his psyche.

It hadn't happen often, but each time it did happen it frightened him. He dreaded this time of year because he knew that the closer he got to that date, November 19, the harder it would be to keep to control the anger he felt. It was useless to try to ignore the date. It was as if his body possessed some independent evil internal clock that tolled more loudly as the date approached.

He knew that Tony was aware of his suppressed hostilities, especially when his mood changed so radically in November. But, Marco made sure Tony never saw him at his worst. He felt sure that Tony didn't suspect the true depth of his anguish. From time to time, his friend gently prodded him to seek help. Marco always deflected Tony's suggestions, sometimes with humor, sometimes more forcefully. He knew he could tame the beast by himself, given enough time. He felt that only weaklings needed outside help to conquer their fears and errant emotions. Certainly after all he had seen in Vietnam, he should be able to handle his own problems. Tony was the only person that seem to understand Marco and to respect his desire to work through his problems unaided.

That was only one of the many reasons why he and Tony had become so close during their almost thirty year friendship. They had shared so many experiences over the years that they instinctively knew how to support each other. They had spent only a few of those thirty years apart. However, the few times it looked like their paths would diverge, fate brought them back together.

They both had grown up in New Jersey, several towns apart. Marco went to Villanova on a ROTC scholarship where he studied computer science. He had wanted to be a soldier for as long as he could remember. As a young boy he was enchanted and inspired by the tales his uncles told him about their experiences in World War II. Their heroic tales of combat thrilled him. They spoke enthusiastically about the satisfaction they got from the liberation of conquered towns and cities and the gratitude of the poor people who suffered under the Nazi yoke. It was these descriptions that also imbued young Marco with the nobility of military service.

He even considered trying to get into West Point. However, he knew he needed an appointment from his senator or congressman. Neither he nor his parents knew anyone who could help them understand and navigate West Point's admission process, so he quickly abandoned his thoughts of entering the Military Academy.

Tony had gone to West Point. They graduated several weeks apart and both were commissioned as infantry officers. They first met at the Infantry Officers Basic Course at Fort Benning. They immediately became good friends because of their Italian and New Jersey backgrounds. The other officers in the course dubbed them the Ravioli Brothers.

Their time as ranger buddies during the nine weeks of Ranger training, cemented the relationship. Ranger buddies shared almost every moment of the training from hand-to-hand combat, mountaineering skills and patrolling in the Delta swamps of the Florida Panhandle. The stress of the training as well as the harsh conditions of the early winter made the emotional and physical support of a buddy critical to the successful completion of the course. Sharing the hardships and rigors of that difficult training spawned many a lifelong friendship. Airborne school followed for both of them. They were both pleasantly surprised to learn that they would be assigned to the same unit in Hawaii, the first Battalion of the 14th infantry.

Their time together in Hawaii before the war intruded on their lives was idyllic. The training was hard, but both Marco and Tony welcomed the opportunity to learn the trade of an infantry officer under the tutelage of many of the combat tested officers and NCOs of the Battalion.

Marco and Tony had rented a small house on the North Shore of Oahu, about 45 minutes from their base at Schofield Barracks. The house became a magnet on weekends for many of their fellow officers, both married and single. Marco recalled fondly the carefree picnics and beach football of those weekends. He always referred to those days in Hawaii as the golden years of his life.

But the distant rumblings of the war in southeast Asia began to intrude more and more on the peaceful and full life they all shared. Marco recalled a Lenin quote he had heard many years before."You may not be interested in war, but war is interested in you." In 1966 when the entire 25th infantry division was deployed to Vietnam, Marco found out just how interested war was in him.

He knew that the extreme contrast between his serene life in Hawaii and the chaotic conditions of combat had also wrought a significant change in his own personality. He longed to be that person of those long gone halcyon days, but knew he could never find his way back there after Vietnam. He had naïvely hoped that when he returned from Vietnam, that he could recapture at least some of the tranquility and peace he so loved from those earlier days. But try as he might, he could never find his way through the darkness of Vietnam to the golden days of Hawaii.

That's why he was so happy when he received the unexpected phone call from Tony. He was hopeful that Tony could help him restore at least some of the fabric of those wonderful days in Hawaii. Marco hoped that Tony's enthusiasm and humor might be just the tonic he needed.

Tony had stayed in the army for several years after returning from Vietnam. He had been stationed at Fort Ord, California. He explained in his phone call that he was leaving the army and returning to New Jersey to help care for his ailing parents who were in a nursing home. He planned to attend Seton Hall University to get an MBA while caring for his parents.

When they finally reunited a few months later, it was just like old times except that the war kept getting between them. It seemed they were two close friends separated by a common experience. Marco felt that Tony was just too willing to talk about his time in Vietnam to anyone who expressed an interest. Sure, most of his stories revolved around the close friends he had served with during the war. However, those stories invariably led to descriptions of events that often made Marco uncomfortable.

That's why Marco had hesitated when Tony proposed that they lived together. After several frank discussions, they were able to define some boundaries that were acceptable to both of them. And, for the most part over the years, their agreement worked remarkably well.

The only real exception to the Vietnam taboo was Justine O'Reilly. She was the Medical Services Officer who had taken care of Tony after he had been wounded. They both recalled with fondness, the soft, bright light she had been in Vietnam. Tony could never explain why he hadn't called Justine when he got home. Marco didn't understand that. After many conversations with Tony, Marco was sure Tony didn't understand it either.

As October faded into November, Marco's mood darkened. He poured himself increasingly into more physical activities like running and weight lifting. At work, he sought out the most vexing complex programming problems in the company. He withdrew from Tony and his own family, spending much of his time alone.

Thankfully, they all had seen him like this before and gave him the distance and solitude they knew he needed. Time had not dimmed the awful memories of Vietnam he still carried. He envied Tony who was able to celebrate his recollections of comradeship and friendship while being able to shut out the difficult times they both suffered in the war. Why, he wondered was God punishing him by leaving him with only the dark side of his time in Vietnam.

CHAPTER THREE

TONY

Tony was concerned about Marco. Ever since Vietnam, Marco has never been good at defending himself. He knew how annoyed his friend was by Henry's constant criticisms of every aspect of his work. He had seen these attacks on several occasions. At first, he let them play out hoping that Marco would pushback forcefully against Henry. Tony suspected that one resolute response from Marco would shatter Henry's fragile and fake aggressive style.

However, in spite of Tony's encouragement to his friend to do just that, Marco remained silent in the face of Henry's unwarranted attacks. Only Tony knew Marco well enough to see the anger building in him. His body became rigid, his hands by his side were rolled into tight fists that flexed involuntarily as he faced Henry. His clenched jaw made his mouth look like a thin brittle straight line across his face.

When Tony returned to New Jersey from his last army assignment on the west coast, he has been surprised by this drastic change in Marco's personality. When they had parted in Vietnam thirty years earlier, Marco had been subdued and introspective. That was true of many of those who had seen combat during their year in Vietnam.

However, once these veterans got back to 'the world', most of them regained the balance they had known before their combat tour. Marco was one of those that seemed frozen in time and unable or unwilling to put the war behind him. That's why Tony was so worried about Marco.

Tony had sensed the change in Marco even during their phone calls. They had seen each other only a few times since Vietnam when Tony had returned to visit his parents. It was obvious to Tony during those brief visits that Marco still carried some unresolved issues from Vietnam. At first, he tried to help Marco to unwind these issues by talking about them. It soon became apparent to Tony that Marco didn't want any help with his problem and he certainly didn't want to talk about Vietnam. Tony soon learned that Marco quickly became annoyed by any probing into the nature of his unresolved issues.

That's why Tony was very hesitant about proposing they live together after he decided to move back to New Jersey. After thinking about it for a long time, Tony decided to propose the idea to Marco. He could tell immediately from Marco's response that he too was uncertain about the suggestion. After some frank discussions, they decided to give it a try.

With very few exceptions, the arrangement had worked remarkably well. The clear boundaries they had set about any discussions of Vietnam was the key to the harmony they enjoyed for the five years they had lived together. Initially, Tony felt that living together would benefit Marco primarily. Marco had seemed so lonely even though he was living in the area he had grown up in and was surrounded by his family. Tony felt that he could provide the support that Marco needed.

He was surprised to find out that it was Marco and his family that had provided the support that he needed, especially after his parents died. They both engaged in an intricate dance which resulted in a friendship stronger than they had enjoyed in Vietnam.

The only topic from their Vietnam days which they both readily recalled with fondness were any stories related to Justine O'Reilly. She had nursed Tony back to health after he had been badly wounded. Marco visited Tony daily when he was in the hospital. Tony later learned that on many of those days, especially in the beginning, when he was heavily sedated, Marco spent many hours sitting and talking to Justine. She seemed to have an infinite capacity to listen to and absorb the problems of the broken men around her. She always had that serene smile, no matter how chaotic things were around her. The young soldiers dubbed her the Mona Lisa of the Pleiku MASH. It was her compassion and caring which gave Tony and Marco the only common ground they could openly share about their time in Vietnam.

Yet, even Justine discussions had boundaries they learned to respect. At first, Marco had pushed Tony to discuss why he had never called Justine when he returned to the states. Tony had made it very clear that any discussion of his relationship with Justine after Vietnam was off limits. He didn't want to talk about it because even he didn't understand it. Justine for him was a mini version of Marco's complex emotions which had been spawned unwillingly by the chaotic and traumatic year they had spent in the war. It just proved to him that they all were affected in many different ways by their time in Vietnam.

He thought often of Justine. He had vowed to himself to track her down and call her on several occasions. He never got around to doing it for many reasons. Their time together in Vietnam now seemed so surreal, almost as if it had happened to someone else. He finally figured out that he didn't call her because he didn't want to know the answer. He didn't want anyone to destroy the memory, even Justine. So, in a way he was just like Marco, with the memory frozen in time and not subject to any postmortem revisions.

However, that's where the similarity between him and Marco ended. They both pretended that Marco had only minor issues, but Tony clearly saw how deeply troubled his friend was. He knew that one day Marco would explode unless Tony could guide him to seek help. Tony spent much of their time together looking for an opportunity to help his troubled comrade.

Marco's memories of Vietnam seem composed of only the dark side of their year in combat. He seemed unable or unwilling to focus on the many positive recollections that Tony had of the comradeship they shared with some of the best people Tony had ever met. He knew that it was his faith that had helped him to overcome the hardships in Vietnam and was helping him still today. He was thankful that God had helped him to forget many of the difficulties and tragedies of the war and left him primarily with the fond memories of his comrades.

CHAPTER FOUR

KATHY

The cafeteria was already filled by the time Marco arrived. He spotted Tony waiting at the entrance to the food service line.

"Where have you been?" Tony asked as Marco approached."Oh never mind," he continued without waiting for an answer." Let's get in line before everything edible is gone."

"Hey Tony, want to try some of my spaghetti and meatballs today?" asked a black man behind the counter.

"See I told you Marco, everything edible is already gone," said Tony loud enough for the server to hear."Today's special is Italian food prepared by a guy who thinks SpaghettiOs is an authentic Italian food."

"Wait a minute man. Let me get this straight," the black man answered obviously enjoying the exchange." You ate ham and lima beans and all that other funky C ration food we all ate in Nam, cold out of a can for a year and you won't eat my spaghetti?"

"Matt," Tony answered feigning seriousness," would you want to eat chitterlings and collard greens that I fixed for you?"

"I see your point man. I'll excuse you and your pies-san there, but hold it down. I still have a ton of this stuff I have to peddle."

Tony continued down the line, bantering with each of the servers in turn. After paying, Tony surveyed the packed cafeteria while he waited for Marco." Let's see who we should grace with our presence today," Tony said more to himself than to Marco."I think we need a little female companionship to go with this meatloaf. What do you think Marco?"

Without waiting for an answer, Tony strode purposely to a table near the center of the cafeteria followed by Marco. The two women sitting at the table looked up only when Tony sat down. "Got room for two more Kathy?" he asked.

"If I said no would you go someplace else?" The dark haired woman asked obviously amused by the intrusion.

"Come on Marco, sit down. I told you they'd like us," Tony said.

Marco hesitated and then sat down in the remaining chair." Marco Covello this is Kathy Gennaro and Debbie Wolfstein, probably the two major reasons I visit the fourth floor so often."

Marco nodded slightly while Tony continued to talk to the girls. He listened halfheartedly while glancing at the two women hoping they didn't notice. Kathy the smaller one, was quite attractive. She wore no makeup which seemed to make her long, black lashes and dark eyes all the more striking. She had two barely noticeable laugh lines around her mouth, which became much bigger, accentuating her smile as she joked with Tony. Marco couldn't help thinking to himself that Kathy was pretty under any circumstances, but when she smiled or laughed, she was radiantly beautiful. Marco had seen her in the halls of the company before, but seeing her up close laughing and joking now made her seem much different, a much more attractive different.

Debbie was almost totally different than Kathy. Her bleached blonde short hair contrasted with her friend's shoulder length black hair. Her blue eyeshadow seemed a little overdone, Marco thought. The only slight similarity between the two girls became apparent when Debbie smiled. She also seemed more attractive when she laughed, something both girls apparently did quite often.

"We just had an interesting encounter with Mr. Clean and his sidekick, Henry," Tony explained. "They sure are truly an unlikely pair."

"Howell wouldn't have anybody work for him who had any balls," Debbie offered.

"Debbie, why is it that you revert to your locker room vocabulary when men are around?" Kathy complained.

"Oh, excuse me. Howell wouldn't have anyone work for him who had the means of producing testosterone. Is that better Kathy?" Debbie retorted." Besides, Henry has an infinite capacity for taking Howell's crap," she continued.

"I'm not so sure Deb," Tony said." I think someday Henry is going to explode. It may not be in our lifetime, but I sure hope I'm around when it happens."

"What you both are overlooking is the fact that Barrington has brought Henry along and promoted him as Barrington rose in the company. Henry's done alright for himself by staying loyal to Barrington," Kathy offered.

"Aa ha, and now we start to get to the heart of this discussion. Because there's one other person at this table who's also been moved up by being loyal to Howell," Debbie added.

"Holy mackerel, did I get promoted after that episode in the computer room this morning? Howell is a nicer guy than I thought," Tony joked.

"No, I hate to disappoint you, but it's Kathy who's been consorting with the enemy. It was Howell who lifted her from the depths of the secretarial pool to the executive floor," Debbie explained.

"Oh no," Tony moaned." You're not indebted in some way to that creep I hope Kathy. Not a nice Italian girl like you. You're not into early American stiffs like Howell are you?"

Before she could answer, Debbie replied,"Well, he tried to get her to the interviewing couch a few times, but thanks to millions of unselfish hours of instruction by heroic and farsighted nuns, Kathy's virginity remains intact."

"enough. Frankly, my virginity or lack thereof, is hardly any of your business," Kathy said a little annoyed." Besides, I'm grateful to Barrington for getting me the chance to work for Mr. Jacobs. Barrington is just nice and felt my work was such that I deserved the promotion."

"Oh please, spare me. Before you it was Boom Boom Vicky. She thought dictation was someone who ruled a small South American country. And rumor has it that she could type like a mink," Debbie added unconcerned by Kathy's scowl.

"Well, if its Bimbo City, how did you get to the fourth floor Debbie?" Tony asked.

"Oh, there's some government rule that says you have to have one Jew on the executive floor of every Goyem organization," Debbie chuckled.

"Oh, what do you know. Here he comes now with Henry in tow for a change. Marco, try to get his shoe size while he's standing here. In case he ever lays a hand on Kathy, I want my Uncle Guido to know how much cement to mix up." Tony said.

"Hi Barrington. Here to renew the discussion of our roots? I think we left off where you were describing the state room your ancestors had on the Mayflower. Barrington's descriptions make the Mayflower seem like the love boat." Tony was clearly ready to resume the taunting of the earlier meeting.

Howell glared at him without speaking before turning to Kathy. "Miss Gennaro, I was hoping your move to the fourth floor would also have elevated your taste in whom you associate with," he sneered. Without waiting for an answer, he strode away leaving Henry in his wake. It was a moment before Henry realized that Howell had left. He stood at the table with a smirk on his face, expecting the encounter to continue.

"Henry, don't look now but your handler is almost out of the cafeteria. You'd better hurry because I'm not sure the leash reaches that far," Tony said.

Henry's smirk disappeared as his head swiveled between the figure of the now vanishing Howell and the group at the table. He took a few steps backward, bumping into another table. He then started walking quickly, then broke into a run in the direction that Howell was last seen.

"My God, what a pair; a snake and a mouse." Debbie was the first to speak."Kathy, how can you let that creep talk to you like that. Now he thinks he's responsible for choosing your friends. Next he'll want to you show you how to eat properly. Who the hell does he think you are, Liza Doolittle?"

"Kathy I think Deb's right. I bet that promotion is going to cost you more than you think," Tony added.

"Leave her alone." Marco said quietly but firmly. It was the first time he had spoken since joining the girls. They all looked at him, surprised by his comment. Marco was flushed with embarrassment when he realized they were all staring at him. He caught Kathy's eyes, then looked away.

"You're right again pal. My friend is a man of few words, but they're always powerful words," Tony said half in jest.

"That Henry is quite a piece of work," Debbie changed the subject."I think he missed his calling. He would've been a perfect East European border guard. You know, one of those guys that sits at the head of a long line with a bunch of rubber stamps. Then after you've waited for hours in the line, he stamps them four or five times and says that your papers are not in order." Debbie pounded the table a few times with her fist to add visual emphasis to her verbal description.

"Well, speaking of papers in order, I ought to be getting back to work," Kathy said. As she stood she looked at Marco who quickly averted his eyes.

CHAPTER FIVE

THE DATE

The headlights of Howell's Mercedes poked ahead in the darkness, managing to barely stay ahead of the speeding car. The long winding drive ended at the top of the hill which was crowned by the large stately clubhouse. Beyond the building, Kathy could see tennis courts and the pool glistening in the moonlight.

As the car rolled to a halt, two young men sprung out of the shadows."Good evening, ma'am. Good evening Mr. Howell." They greeted the couple almost in unison as they opened each door. Kathy waited as Howell turned over his key to the valet before taking her arm and walking up the steps to the clubhouse. Kathy had heard a lot about the Heritage Hills Country Club from a guy she had dated in high school. He had been a lifeguard at the club and had told her many stories about the country club and its members. She had always been fascinated by his stories and would ask him a lot of questions about what he saw and did. She had always felt that she had dated Doug a little longer than she wanted to, mainly because of her interest in his stories of the 'Life and Times of Heritage Hills Country Club.' Once school started and he ended his lifeguard job, their romance had cooled quickly.

Now, here she was about to enter the clubhouse of the most prestigious country clubs in northern New Jersey. Doug had worked at the country club for three years, and had never been in the clubhouse. That thought seemed strangely to give Kathy a sense of finality about her relationship with Doug which she had considered over many years before.

As anxious as Kathy was to enter the clubhouse, she knew she was slowing down as they approached the entrance. Howell sensed her reticence and said," Don't let this place spook you Kathy. It's really just a glorified restaurant where the elite of Essex County come to try to impress one another." He tightened his grip on her arm and led her through the double oak doors.

Kathy was angry at herself for showing that she was intimidated. She gave a little nervous laugh and allowed Howell to lead her into the huge foyer. A large, beautiful chandelier sparkled brightly, giving the room an air of gaiety in spite of the dark paneled walls. From there they passed into a large hallway lined with plaques.

"Come here Kathy I want to show you something," said Howell as he nudged her toward one of the many hanging plaques. He let go of her arm and walked quickly ahead, pointing to what he wanted her to see.

As she approached it, she could see it read in large letters, 'Club Tennis Champion'. Aligned on the plaque were many smaller plates indicating the years and names of the champions. Howell was proudly pointing to one of the inscribed plates which read, 'Barrington Howell 1978'.

Howell looked at Kathy expectantly, as he continued to point at his name." Oh that's wonderful, Barrington," Kathy said without enough enthusiasm. She knew it was one of the things she found she disliked about Howell in the short time she had known him. He was a paradox. On the one hand, he was self-assured and confident and she liked that. However, he was always fishing for compliments and he seemed to have an insatiable need to be told how wonderful he was. She knew that was what Henry's primary function was and it appeared he had an infinite capacity to oblige his boss." That's really wonderful, Barrington," Kathy tried to be more enthusiastic a second time.

"I'll tell you about it over dinner. The final match was a real battle. Almost the whole club turned out for it," Howell seemed not to notice her lack of interest. He took her arm again and continued down the hallway.

They emerged into a large dining room with floor-to-ceiling windows lining one wall."Good evening, Mr. Howell. Nice to see you again," the hostess greeted him."I have your table ready if you'll follow me."

They were seated at a table near one of the windows. In the moonlight, Kathy could see well manicured flower beds and walkways leading out to the golf course."Barrington, this is beautiful. I can only see it a little in the darkness, but I'll bet the grounds are gorgeous," Kathy said.

"Nothing is more gorgeous than you are tonight, Kathy," Howell said as he reached across the table to grasp Kathy's hands. She flushed a little and pulled her hands away.

"I'm not sure I can handle this place and you being so suave Barrington," she said with a smile.

"I was counting on that," Howell said with a little laugh.

* * * *

"Another glass of wine, Kathy?" Howell asked as the dishes were being cleared.

"No thank you, I think I've had enough Barrington," Kathy answered. She was a little concerned when he ordered a scotch for himself. She had only had one glass of wine in spite of Howell's insistence that she have more. He had finished the rest of the wine bottle and had now switched to scotch. Except for a slight slurring of his speech, the only other effect the alcohol had on him was that he seemed to be considerably more talkative.

"You must love it out here, Barrington. Everything is so beautiful and well cared for. And these people do such a good job of making you feel special," Kathy gushed.

"Oh it is kind of nice out here. My family has belonged here for ages. I spent a lot of hours at that pool when I was younger. My mother used to dump us out here while she played golf or bridge," Howell said somewhat flatly.

"Tell me about your family Barrington," Kathy said.

"Oh, there's not much to tell," he said as he surveyed the dining room. He paused for a moment, then continued." My father is a retired doctor. My older brother, true to my parents' expectations, became a doctor and is now the head of surgery in a Boston hospital. My younger sister is a psychiatrist in Denver. As you can see, I'm the only one that broke the chain."

"Well, you're certainly successful in your own right. You're a top executive in a major insurance company," Kathy said sensing some hostility in Howell's family description.

"Yes, but I'm not a doctor." Howell fairly hissed the words."Even here, anyone not a doctor is a second-class citizen. No one calls you a second class citizen, but it shows up in a thousand little ways. In the men's locker room we all have name tags on our lockers. Mine says Barrington Howell. My father's said Dr. Howell. Only doctors have their titles. Why shouldn't I have MIS Director Howell or Big Insurance Guy Howell on my locker?"

Kathy couldn't conceal the surprise on her face. It was hard to believe that Howell was getting emotional about something as trivial as the name on his locker.

He sighed and said sadly," I'm sure you don't understand Kathy. However, if you have grown up as a non-doctor in a doctor family, you'd understand. On the other hand, if I had become a doctor, I might not have met you."

"And if you hadn't met me, I'd be home right now where I should be pretty soon since tomorrow is a work day and I have an early meeting with Mr. Jacobs," Kathy joked.

"Oh you career women are all alike. Just one more drink Kathy and we'll be on our way."

"Howell, this has been a wonderful evening. Let's not spoil it by negotiating when I get home. You agreed to get me home by midnight. Besides, just because you helped me get my job with Mr. Jacobs, doesn't entitle you to help me get fired from it," Kathy joked hoping to relieve what was becoming a tense situation.

Howell stared intensely at her for a second then said," Okay you win Kathy. I can never say no to a beautiful woman." He got up from the table, clumsily rattling the coffee cups. Kathy waited for him to pull out her chair but he was already starting out of the dining room. She got up, looking around somewhat embarrassed, and followed behind Howell.

* * * *

"I've always liked this neighborhood. The houses are so neat and clean," Howell said as they approached Kathy's house.

"*Small, neat and clean is what he really means,*" Kathy thought to herself. Howell had been quiet on the ride home, so she welcomed even his snide comment.

"One thing you can say about immigrants as they keep their neighborhoods clean," Howell added.

"*That's as close as Barrington can come to a compliment about non-wasps,*" Kathy thought.

"I don't think these people think of themselves as immigrants. These are hard-working people who are proud of what they've accomplished," Kathy said not wanting to antagonize Howell anymore than he already was.

The Mercedes glided to a stop in front of Kathy's parents' modest house. Howell turned off the car and the lights and turned to Kathy. His hand brushed against her breast as he reached for her and gave her a wet kiss. She was so surprised by his sudden move that it took her a moment before she pushed him away.

"I have to go in Barrington," she said opening the car door."Thank you for a lovely evening," she said flatly.

"I hope we can do this again sometime, when you're allowed to stay out later," Howell said sarcastically.

Kathy pretended she didn't hear him and walked quickly to the front door. Howell's Mercedes roared away with a squeal of tires.

She watched the Mercedes recede in the distance before she unlocked the door. As she looked into the living room she could see the blue glow of the TV which cast dim shadows around the room as the picture changed. As Kathy's eyes became accustomed to the dark, she could see her father asleep in his chair. It was a worn recliner that her father had had for as long as she could remember. As she approached him, she could see that his glasses had fallen onto the newspaper that he still clutched to his chest.

Kathy looked at her father for a moment, thinking that he had been looking older lately. Since he became bald when he was young, he had always seemed somewhat ageless to Kathy. Lately, she had noticed that he acted and looked more like an old man. *"He's just been working too hard,"* Kathy thought to herself.

She gently removed his glasses and the newspaper and put them on a table near the chair. She smiled when she noticed the Italian headlines of 'Il Travatore', her father's favorite newspaper. It always antagonized Kathy's mother when he read the Italian newspaper, so he waited until his wife went to bed before reading it. His ability to get much past the first page before falling asleep

had diminished considerably recently. Yet, the uneasy truce with his wife continued as long as the ritual was followed.

Her parents were so different, Kathy reflected as she looked down at her sleeping father. He had been born in Italy, but had come to the United States when he was four. Her mother had been born in the United States to Italian immigrant parents. Kathy's father didn't care much about material things while her mother lamented often about what they didn't have. Her father had been handsome when he was young, Kathy knew from early pictures. However, now he wasn't too concerned about his appearance and joked about having to look like an elderly Italian, bald with a paunch. Her mother, still trim and attractive even with graying hair, was always well groomed. "*So much alike and yet so different*", she mused. Much of the difference seemed to revolve around their views of their ethnic backgrounds. Her father was proud of his Italian roots while her mother was anxious to 'melt' and to become as American as possible." *I guess opposites do attract, I just don't know if they continue to attract,*" Kathy thought.

She gently shook her father and whispered," Pop, it's time to go to bed."

"Oh, hi baby. What time is it?" He asked sleepily.

"It's a little after midnight and time for you to go to bed. Let me help you upstairs," Kathy said as she is assisted him in getting out of the chair.

They walked arm in arm up the stairs." Did you have a nice time tonight?" Her father yawned.

"It was very nice. Heritage Hills Country Club is gorgeous. I wish I could take you there someday Pop."

"Nah, I wouldn't want to go. I hear their bocce ball courts are not very good," he said with a grin." Thanks for bringing me up, I'll see you in the morning."

"I love you Pop," Kathy said as she kissed him on the cheek. She continued down the hall to her own room, closing the door gently behind herself.

As she started to undress, her mother came into the room." Well, how was it?" she gushed.

"It was nice," Kathy answered.

"Nice! You go to one of the most elegant places in New Jersey with one of the most eligible bachelors in this town and all you can tell me is that it was nice! It's like having Cinderella tell you she had a nice time at the ball. What a great fairytale writer you would have made."

"Mom, I'm not Cinderella and I didn't go to a ball. I had a dinner date with a guy from work like a million other women tonight. Somehow, I don't think that there are many of those other women or their mothers who are equating that to a Cinderella experience."

"Oh come on Kathy, let your old mother live vicariously for a moment through you," her mother tried to joke sensing Kathy's irritation.

"Well, if you have to know and you want to put it in a Cinderella framework, Barrington turned into a pumpkin. He got somewhat inebriated and then a little testy when I insisted on being home by midnight."

"Oh come on Kathy, I can't believe a guy like Barrington Howell would get drunk, especially at his country club in front of his friends.

I'm sure he was just relaxed and that speaks well for you and your ability to make him feel comfortable on a first date."

"I can't believe you. You weren't even there and yet you side with a stranger over your own daughter as to how he acted. Why is it so hard for you to believe that wealthy men at a country club can act just as stupidly as poor guys at the corner tavern?" Kathy said angrily.

"Honey I'm not siding with anyone. I was just anxious for you to have a nice time this evening and I guess I'm a little disappointed it didn't work out that way," Kathy's mother said softly.

"Why? Why, mom. Why was this date so important to you? You talked about it all last week and now you seem more disappointed than I am." Kathy said angrily.

"It's not that important to me Kathy. It's important to you and I know you don't realize how important it is to you. Barrington Howell represents a chance for you to elevate yourself, to meet new and exciting people and get beyond the limits this neighborhood has set for you. I'm not saying you have to marry him. I'm only saying give him a chance to introduce you to his circle of friends who, in turn, will introduce you to their friends. Then at least you'll have the ability to compare and choose among different lifestyles," Kathy's mother persisted.

"Mom, there's nothing wrong with the lifestyle of this neighborhood. I grew up here and I love it." Kathy was less angry now.

"I am not saying it's bad or wrong. I am just saying you'll never know if you don't give men like Barrington a chance to show you what other choices you could have. Look at your brother Rick. He dated

Angela all through high school. They married and now they have a little house three blocks away and a lifetime of financial worries."

"Mom, Rick and Angela have a wonderful marriage. I don't know any two people as much in love as they are," Kathy said.

"Honey, I didn't mean they're not happy. But, how do we know Ricky couldn't have been just as happy or even happier with someone else. It's just as easy to fall in love with someone rich as it is someone poor. Poor Rick works so hard and has almost nothing. And those poor kids. I wish I could afford to buy them the clothes and toys I know Rick would like to get them. But, he's chosen and you're right he's happy. But you're different. You've always been different. When you were young and I took you to dancing class, all of those little rich girls liked you. Do you remember little Sarah Jenkins? She called you for years after those dancing classes. In high school, you were friendlier with the girls from uptown than you were with the girls from around here."

"And how about you Mom? Do you wish you had chosen differently?" Kathy asked, immediately regretting the cruelty of the question and not wanting to hear the answer.

"Oh honey, I really didn't have the choices you have. Things were different then. Your father is a good man and he has always been good to me. But I'd be lying if I said that I didn't think about what might have been from time to time. I think everyone dreams like that as they get older." Kathy's mother said quickly, obviously wanting to change the subject.

Kathy persisted."Is that why you don't like it when Pop speaks Italian and why you wouldn't let him go visit Uncle Bruno in Italy? Since you couldn't or wouldn't change your choice, you tried to change who you chose as much as possible. I'm beginning to under-stand you a lot more."

"Kathy, I think you're making more of this conversation than you should," Kathy's mother said defensively." I'm only trying to show you that you don't have to and shouldn't make any important decisions about your life until you've explored all the choices."

"I'm tired mom. I want to go to sleep now," Kathy said with an air of finality.

"Honey, someday you'll understand that I want only the best for you and that I was only trying to help you avoid potential mis-takes." Kathy's mother leaned down and kissed her. She turned the light off and left the room, gently closing the door behind herself.

CHAPTER SIX

THE MATCH

"Come on Kathy, you can tell me a little something about the big date last night," Debbie implored.

"Debbie you and I both know that if I tell you anything about last night, you'll only embellish it and by the time I hear the story again it won't bear any resemblance to what I told you. So I'm better off not saying anything and denying everything," Kathy said with a grin." I know better than to tell anything to the biggest yenta in New Jersey," she added.

"I hate when shiksas like you use Yiddish. I'm sorry I ever told you those words. There's nothing worse than to being beaten with your own material," Debbie was smiling."However, if you don't tell me something, I'll be forced to make up a story. I can't let my fans down. And you know, I can conjure up a juicier story than that boring WASP, Barrington Howell was capable of doing. What will it be Miss Shiksa Queen?"

"Okay, Debbie you win. But if you distort the facts, I'll have my mother cut you off from your lasagna supply. You'll be back to SpaghettiOs before you know it," Kathy said threateningly.

"Well well, Marco. Look who's here again. Kathy and Debbie," Tony's voice boomed out from several feet away." They're trying to act demure but I know better. Why else would they always choose a table right on the route they know we take in the cafeteria? But then again, I like forward, liberated women," Tony said as he sat down. Marco stood for a second, not knowing whether to join Tony in his intrusion on the girls. "Come on Marco, sit down or you'll disappoint these girls. They have probably used up almost all of their lunch hour waiting for us," Tony added.

"Why don't you buzz off DeJulio?" Debbie countered,"We're going to use words with more than one syllable and it'll be boring for you not being able to understand what we're talking about," Debbie added with a grin.

"You should have seen my friend Marco over there," Tony pretended he didn't hear Debbie." He's trying to pass for American, but he always blows it and gives away his immigrant roots. He waited in line until there were plenty of people within earshot. Then he says in his best, most precise WASP voice, I'll have the Virginia ham, mashed potatoes, green beans and a nica, bigga glass of milk." Tony nearly spit out the final words because he was laughing so hard.

Marco looked a little embarrassed, but was laughing as well, obviously amused by his friend's fictitious description of him.

"Hey Don Rickles, knock it off. I was about to get the lowdown on Kathy's big date with Barrington last night when you launched into your schtick. Cool it or we'll never learn how the King of Bland charmed our little Kathy here," Debbie said firmly.

"Whoa, this is hot stuff. I didn't know you were dating Howell Kathy. I don't learn anything anymore since I let my subscription to the National Inquirer lapse," Tony said in mock disappointment.

"Well, you'd better renew your subscription because you're not going to hear anything about it at this table," Kathy said as she glared at Debbie.

"Well, I'll just ask Howell himself. He's coming this way," Tony said matter-of-factly.

"Oh my God Kathy, he's coming over here," Debbie added.

Kathy, not knowing whether to believe either of them, turned around to see Barrington striding purposefully toward them, followed closely by Henry." If either of you make any kind of smart comment about my date last night, I'll kill you." Kathy fairly hissed the threat as she turned back around." And I am not joking."

"Kathy, I'm disappointed to find you with these troublemakers two days in a row," Howell said as he approached the table.

"And what are you, the cafeteria monitor Howell?" Tony asked.

"Why don't you come over and sit with me. I want to talk to you Kathy," Howell said ignoring Tony's taunt.

"How come you're not eating. Did they run out of caviar already?" Tony persisted trying to get a response from Howell.

Howell turned to Tony, glared and said," Yeah, the only thing they have left is some wop food and I wouldn't eat that shit if I were starving."

It was obvious that the bantering had turned ugly. Everyone at the table sensed the hostility between the two men." Listen Miles

Standish, I've had about all the ethnic crap out of you that I'm going to take," Tony stood up and faced Howell.

Debbie stood up between the two men and said," Come on you guys. Go to a neutral corner and act like adults instead of two 12-year-olds."

"Yeah, Debbie's right. Besides, I wouldn't want to get any of your blue blood on my new red tie. I paid twenty dollars for this tie and as much as I would enjoy punching you in the mouth, it isn't worth ruining my new tie," Tony said as he sat down.

"I don't know why you're so worried about staining that cheap tie. The first time you eat spaghetti, it'll be covered with tomato sauce. That's why you buy red ties isn't it, DeJulio? Because you don't know how to use a napkin yet." It was obvious Howell was not ready to end the confrontation.

"Howell, why don't you lay off. Don't you have a Sons of the American Revolution meeting you should be going to?" Debbie asked." Besides if we want to have a red, white and blue contest, these guys would win hands down. They spent a year of their lives in Vietnam while you were home bitching about income taxes. What do you think Isaiah Barrington or Jeremiah Howell or whoever your ancestor was would think of that?"

Howell responded while looking at Tony and Marco." They'd think what the rest of this country thinks. That anyone who went over there was too dumb to see what a big waste it was. It doesn't surprise me that these two losers participated in the only military effort we lost. Actually, I'm surprised they were smart enough to get back to the US without getting killed.

Even before Howell finished, Marco leaped from his seat, pushed Tony aside and threw Howell roughly against the wall. With his left hand, Marco grabbed the taller man around the throat while he locked his right-hand menacingly preparing to strike. For a moment, he glared at Howell with a hatred which was clearly visible to everyone at the table.

Marco's swift movement had surprised everyone in the room. The sudden movement and the noise of Howell hitting the wall caused the cafeteria to grow silent. After a few seconds, Marco released his hold and strode swiftly from the cafeteria. Howell still surprised by the sudden and swift attack, took a few moments to regain his breath. He swallowed nervously a few times. He was obviously shaken as he attempted to straighten his tie and shirt with trembling hands.

"Your buddy's gone too far this time DeJulio," Howell said, his voice higher pitched than normal." Even that liberal faggot in Personnel can't look past this assault on a manager."

"My guess is that the liberal faggot in Personnel and the big guy, Mr. Donlon would both like to know about the comments made by one of our senior managers that provoked Marco," Tony answered.

The noise and activity in the cafeteria slowly returned to its previous level. Howell and Tony kept looking at each other, seeming both to realize that they were at a standoff. Neither of them seemed willing to end the confrontation, yet neither wanted to escalate it further.

Debbie finally broke the silence." Why don't you and Marco meet in the parking lot and duke it out Howell. That way the personnel faggot or Mr. Donlon need not get involved. And that way no one's lunch would get ruined by seeing your head cracked open."

"Nah, I don't think you'd like those odds Howell. The only reason Marco paused here today was because he was debating whether to drive your nose bone into your brain or whether to stick his finger into your windpipe and rip your sternum down to your bellybutton. He learned some things in Ranger school that I can't get him to forget. It's like riding a bike. You don't have to do it every day to be able to use it when you need it," Tony's playful, sarcastic tone was returning.

Howell gulped visibly. He moved his hand unconsciously to his throat." I'll tell you what Howell. I think Debbie's got a good point here," Tony continued."Since this all happened so publicly, I think we need to bring this to some kind of conclusion. If this had been 200 years ago, you and Marco could've had a duel and he would have gone on with his life without having to listen to your ethnic crap anymore after putting a bullet in your brain. But, we're all too sophisticated for that, so we have to figure out another way for Marco to trash you."

Tony paused for dramatic effect before resuming." I know, how about a boxing match. I know Marco would like that. He was brigade boxing champ in the army. I'm sure he'd spot you the 20 or 30 pounds you have on him. Besides, the company picnic was kind of dull this year and a boxing match would be sure to attract a lot of folks who don't attend company functions," Tony ended with a grin. Everyone at the table looked at Howell, awaiting his reply. Henry who was standing behind Howell, took several steps backward as if to disassociate himself from the proceedings.

Howell looked from Kathy to Tony several times before he answered." Although I'm sure the gladiator aspect of this whole thing appeals to you DeJulio, this is the 20th Century. We ought to settle disputes like this in a more civilized manner. I propose you arrange a tennis match between your friend and me. If you're looking for a spectacle, a tennis match would appeal to a wider range of people more than some barbaric, bloody contest." Howell's composure was obviously returning. Henry, sensing the return of his companion's confidence, retraced his steps so that he was once again standing close to Howell.

"Yeah, a tennis match. Marco played tennis in high school. You got it. Debbie we'll arrange the time and place. Make it big enough for the whole company to watch Deb, because I think there are a lot of people who want to see this bozo get his due."

"Tell your friend I'll see him on the court," Howell said with a smirk. He turned and walked quickly out of the cafeteria followed by Henry.

* * * *

"A tennis match? Tony, what's the matter with you? I haven't played tennis in years. Howell will make a fool of me." Marco was as upset as Tony had seen him for quite sometime.

"Pal, tennis is like riding a bicycle. You never forget how to play. It'll come back to you with a little practice," Tony tried to reassure Marco." All you have to do is direct half of the intensity I saw in that cafeteria to your tennis match with Howell and it will be no contest."

"That was pretty dumb today. I vowed a long time ago not to let that turkey get my goat. I've done fine all these years in spite of all the ethnic crap he's given us. But, when I cracked, I had to do it in front of the whole company. I don't know what's the matter with me." Marco lamented.

"Marco, we both know what happened in the cafeteria today," Tony said seriously."That explosion has been waiting to happen for a long time. Now that it's happened, you and I need to take advantage of the opportunity to talk about it."

"Tony, I don't need any of your psychoanalytic crap. What happened was that an asshole who has been pushing me for a long time finally pushed me too far. It's that simple. If you're going to give me any of that bullshit about suppressed feelings or delayed stress syndrome I'm getting out of here. You and I have been over that garbage a hundred times. How long will it be before you believe that I put Vietnam behind me?" Marco said coldly.

"When you can talk about it without getting pissed off or emotional, Marco that's when," Tony persisted.

"Tony," Marco's tone was now more hostile and accusing."It was a bullshit year. It wasn't a class trip or a visit to the zoo. It was a sorry ass, bullshit wasted year. Why would I want to spend any time talking about that? I think you're the screwed up one for wanting to talk about it so much. I just want to forget it." Marco's voice was rising.

Tony moved to Marco's side and put his arm around his friends shoulder." Yeah, you're right pal. That was a long time ago, a different world. Who needs that shit anyhow?" Tony smiled broadly. " We got a big fish to fry, mainly Mr. Howell and how you're going to humiliate him. I can see the headlines now, '*Marco Covello Humiliates Barrington Howell.' Millions of common folks who have been crapped on by Howell rejoice. Hollywood to do movie version starring Pee-wee Herman.'*

"You asshole," Marco said as he pushed Tony aside." What's really going to happen is that I'm going to look like the jerk. I'll probably never be able to show my face around work after you get done managing my career."

"Well, I can see the thought of millions of dollars and a Hollywood contract didn't motivate you much. How about kicking Howell's butt and winning over the heart of that sweet Kathy Gennaro?" Tony asked.

"I have to confess, if trying had anything to do with winning her heart, I'd be killing myself to try to win," Marco said half in jest." But, tennis is a finesse game. The less emotions the better. That's why the English love it so much. They only have to say bravo once at the end of the match." Marco smiled obviously much more relaxed." Besides there's the question of the Mercedes and the country club which has to be pretty heady stuff for a girl like Kathy."

"Don't be so sure pal. Underneath that thin veneer of a lady, beats the heart of an Italian peasant just like you and me." Tony reassured him." Besides, all of this is conjecture if you don't beat Howell. That's the first order of business."

"Tony, I can't beat Howell. I haven't played tennis since high school and he probably plays every weekend at his club, "Marco said.

"Don't worry pal. I have it all figured out. I went to personnel this afternoon and put us on a two-week vacation starting tomorrow. We'll start out for Sea Girt to visit Freddy. He's a tennis coach for a high school down there. You'll work out a few weeks with him and then we'll come back here to take on Howell. Yeah, a few weeks with fast Freddy and you'll be able to win Wimbledon," Tony said smugly.

"I can't believe you. You've always been a little flaky, but now you've gone off the deep end," Marco said." Henry will never let me leave on such short notice."

"Wrong again garlic breath. Blakely in personnel called Henry while I was in the personnel office. Henry was very cooperative. I suspect he was helpful because Howell doesn't want anyone to think he did anything to prevent you from putting forth your best effort. That smug S.O.B," Tony said.

"Well, Freddy won't have the time to spend with me. He's got to teach school," Marco countered.

"Still wrong, linguine lips. I already called Freddy and he says he has a light schedule this semester. He can spend a few hours with you, then give you some drills to do while he teaches. Then he can spend more time and continue the process over again. No more screwing around. It's a done deal. We leave at dawn tomorrow. You better go and pack," Tony said with an air of finality.

* * * *

"Ta ta Ta ta Ta ta," Marco awakened to Tony's poor imitation of a bugle." Rise and shine soldier. We have a long trip ahead of us today," Tony yelled." If you're not out of that bed in one minute, I'm dumping the mattress and you on the floor."

"Come on Tony, I'm tired. I'm not kidding leave me alone." Marco pleaded.

"Thirty seconds soldier and you get dumped on the barracks floor. We have an important operation planned and we have no time to screw around." Tony persisted.

Realizing that Tony was serious, Marco opened his eyes. He saw his friend hovering over him wearing his old army bush hat and jungle fatigues.

"Fifteen seconds soldier," Tony moved closer to the bed.

"Okay, okay I'll get up. What time is it anyway?" Marco asked.

"It's 5 o'clock," Tony answered.

"Oh crap Tony. Why do we have to get up so early?" Marco groaned.

"Because we have to cross the line of departure in 30 minutes and then we have to cross phase line blue at 7:30. After you wake up a little more, I'll fill you in on the other control points of the operation," Tony said seriously.

"You know, you really are screwed up Tony." Marco said as he got out of bed.

"You have a choice pal. You can pack your stuff in a suitcase or this duffel bag. I've already packed my stuff in my own duffel bag. We have to travel light during this operation," Tony admonished.

"I'm taking a suitcase. If I go on this trip, I'm going to be civilized. You can regress all you want, but I am going to live like a human being," Marco replied.

"I was afraid creature comforts would take over your body someday Marco. You remember how we were warned in Ranger school about getting too soft. If you become much more of a pansy,

I may have to write to the Ranger department to have them rescind your Ranger tab," Tony said with a smile." If you have to take a shower, I don't want you to use any hot water so you can start to harden yourself for this operation."

"Screw you Captain DeJulio." Marco said as he walked into the bathroom and slammed the door.

"And I suppose C-rations on the lawn is out of the question for breakfast," Tony yelled through the door." I'll even heat them with some sterno."

CHAPTER SEVEN

TRAINING

The car sped along the Garden State Parkway into the increasing daylight. Marco and Tony had been driving for almost 3 hours. The congested northern New Jersey landscape had given way to the flat sandy terrain of the coastal area. Since arriving in the mid point of the state there had been very little traffic.

Tony thought for a moment, as if considering Marco's comments an opinion of some third-party then proudly said," You know pal I think you're right. I don't think even I realize what a great story teller I am. But seriously, the women out here are tough. They could chew you up and spit you out before you even know you've been had."

"Oh BS, Tony. Women are women," Marco sounded unconvinced.

"Okay pal, we're looking for Atlantic Avenue," Tony said as he exited the parkway." This is Sea Girt, one of the neat little towns on the New Jersey shore. I used to visit my aunt and uncle in a neighboring town every year when I was a kid. The New Jersey shore is one of the world's best kept secrets. It's beautiful and has more women per square foot of sand than any other beach area."

"Okay, we're coming up on Atlantic Tony," Marco said.

"There it is, 1152. I remember it now. I came out to visit Freddy a few years after we got home," Tony recalled. The car slowed as he pulled in front of a small wooden framed house. The outside light was on, revealing a rocking chair and the swinging sofa on the small porch in front of the house."There he is in the chair by the window, reading the newspaper," Tony said excitedly as he got out of the car. Without waiting for Marco, he ran quickly up to the porch." Yoo-hoo, Mrs. Bronson, can little Freddy come out and play?" Tony yelled in a falsetto voice trying to imitate a child.

Without moving his newspaper, Freddy answered also in a falsetto voice." No he can't, I don't like him to play with assholes."

"Get out here you turkey before I come in there and dust that filthy room with your body," Tony yelled through the open window.

Through the window, Marco could see Freddy jump up from his chair. The door was flung open and Freddie leaped on Tony who was surprised by the speed and vigor of the attack." Airborne," Freddy yelled as he pulled Tony to the ground. As they rolled around on the front lawn, Marco walked cautiously near the wrestling duo." I can't believe you guys," Marco said seriously." Two grown men and you still greet each other like two Neanderthals back from a hunt."

"Wait Fred, I think I've cut myself on something here in the grass," Tony said seriously.

"Oh my God, you have Tony. You're bleeding," Freddy answered with alarm.

Marco moved closer to the two men, trying to see the wound in the darkness. As he got closer, both men reached up and dragged him to the ground."He's always been a sucker for a sad story," Tony said as he and Freddie wrestled Marco to the ground.

After a few minutes of strenuous horseplay, all three men lay on their backs breathing heavily. Freddy was the first to stand. He pulled each of his friends up, put one arm around each and said soberly," Welcome home."

CHAPTER EIGHT

CHUCK AND THE WALL

Marco was sweating in the cool autumn afternoon, He had been hitting balls fired by a ball machine for almost two hours. He could see Tony and Freddie conferring just outside the tennis court while they watched him. Marco could tell something was up by the serious discussion the other two men were having.

"Okay Marco, good job," Tony said as he walked onto the tennis court." You're not Jimmy Connors yet, but I see a lot of improvement," he added as he extended a towel towards Marco.

"Yeah, nice job Marco. I know you've been working hard these last two days," Freddie said as he joined them.

"Okay, what's up you two?" Marco asked suspiciously." I watched that summit meeting you guys were having for the last half hour and I know something's up. My guess is that you guys know what I know, that this whole scheme isn't going to work."

"Oh no pal, that's not it at all," Tony said defensively.

"Actually Marco, you've been doing great. It's just that we don't have a lot of time and at the rate I'm helping you it just won't work. If I had a few months or even one month, I know I could get you to the point where you'd kick what's his name's ass. But, we don't have that much time. You need one of those concentrated tennis clinics. This part-time coaching I'm doing just isn't getting the job done," Freddie said putting his arm around Marco.

"Yeah and these two days haven't been wasted 'cause they got you into condition thanks to Freddy's ten hour schedules," Tony added.

"Well, I think we gave it a good try. I just have to grow a beard, get dark glasses, change my voice and name so that I can sneak back into my home town after my best friend set up this dumb match. It's really not that bad though, I'll probably be able to surface in 20 or 30 years," Marco said sarcastically.

"Oh no pal, you don't understand. We've just begun to fight. Fred gave me the name of the best tennis clinic in the country and we're going there to get you enrolled and transferred into one of the premier tennis players within three thousand miles," Tony said enthusiastically.

"You guys have to be crazy. Fred, I expected you to have some common sense about this. I've never heard of a world class tennis training facility in southern New Jersey. Where is this place any-how?" Marco asked.

"Dallas, Texas here we come," Tony and Fred said in unison.

"Tony how do you do this? Now you've changed Freddy's life. How many people are you going to get wrapped up in this cockama-mie scheme?" Marco said in exasperation.

"Only Chuck and Tom, who we will pick up along the way," Tony said with a grin."Now come along little buddy, we have to pack and leave tonight. We're meeting Chuck late tonight in DC. I can use the time in the car to brief you on how to handle DC women." Tony said as he guided Marco off the tennis court.

* * * *

Marco could see the Washington Monument off in the distance, illuminated against the overcast night sky." That's really something. The Washington monument looks just like it does in all those photographs. Before we take off tomorrow, Chuck is going to take us on a short tour of all of the monuments. We'll get to see the Lincoln Memorial and maybe walk to the top of the Washington Monument. And we'll see the wall," Tony's voice trailed off.

"Yeah, we'll see the wall," Freddy said quietly. The trio rode on in silence until they crossed over a bridge into nearby Georgetown.

"Okay you guys, we're looking for Chuck's hangout, a bar called, the 'Colonial Soldier," Tony said breaking the silence.

"There it is Tony," Freddy said."It looks like the kind of yuppie hangout our yuppie friend would be in. Turn down one of the side streets and park. That'll give us a chance to walk up and do a recon before we go in."

After parking the car, the three men walked up the brightly lit street. Even though it was close to 10 o'clock, the streets of Georgetown were filled with numerous window shoppers and strollers.

"This is unbelievable. It's 10 o'clock on a Wednesday night and this town is jumping. Back in New Jersey right now everyone's asleep," Tony said in mock amusement.

Tony, Marco and Freddy walked into the bar and paused near the entrance trying to get their eyes adjusted to the dim light. After a few minutes of peering around, Tony made his way through the crowd to the bar." Hey pal, where can I find Chuck Saunders?" he yelled to the bartender over the din of the crowd.

"He's at his regular table in the back corner probably giving free legal advice," the bartender yelled back.

Tony motioned to his two friends and all three pushed their way to the rear of the bar." There's the turkey, surrounded by women," Freddie said in disgust.

Chuck saw them at almost the same time and quickly left the table and made his way toward them. He gripped the hand of each of his friends in turn. "Boy, it's good to see you guys again. I'm really glad you called me Tony. I've been warming up to call you guys for about six months now. Somehow, I never seemed to get around to it. I'm glad you set this deal up. Getting back together is long overdue. Come on over to my table, I want you to meet a couple of nice girls."

"Carol, Kelly, these are a few of my army buddies, Tony, Marco and Fred," Chuck said as they arrived back at the table.

Both girls were attractive and well-dressed."It's always nice to meet Chuck's friends, especially if they're not lawyers," Carol said with a smile.

"I didn't know you were in the army Chuck," the other girl said seriously.

"Not only was he in the army, but he was one heckuva soldier," Tony volunteered." Why one time in Vietnam..." Tony stopped in mid sentence when he saw Chuck roll his eyes and shake his head.

"The army and Vietnam. Boy, there's a lot I don't know about you Chuck. But, we'll have plenty of time to explore the many mysteries of your life I hope," Kelly said."Right now, I think Carol and I need to get going. Besides, if you guys are anything like my dad and his army buddies you have a lot of stories that need to be told again. Nice meeting you."

"You girls don't have to leave. If you go, it's going to force us to tell the truth," Tony said with a smile.

"Thanks, but we do have to leave. If you're going to be in town for a while, maybe we can all get together and you can give me the real scoop on my mysterious friend," Kelly said as she left the table.

The four men watched as the women disappeared into the crowd." Two knock-out women sitting with this turkey and he lets them get away and trades them for three ugly guys. I think that grenade did more than fill up your legs with metal Chuck," Freddy said derisively.

"Those girls are great. But I have to tell you that this town is filled with great girls. By tomorrow night, I'll have you convinced that the Founding Fathers knew what they were doing when they put our nation's capitol here," Chuck said with a smile. "But a word of caution. These D.C. women are sophisticated, intelligent and strong women. They won't be easily fooled by you New Jersey bozos.

"Not to worry Gorgonzola breath. Marco and I have been raised in a state where a woman could carve you up verbally and leave you for dead without you even knowing it happened."

"Why would I think this is another of Tony's exaggerations? " Chuck said looking at Freddie

"I kid you not. Well let me give you a good example Mr. Wiseguy by way of a story which I personally know to be true." Tony said seriously." A disbelieving bozo from the Midwest just like you was visiting his eastern friend who tried to warn him like I am trying to warn you. Well, this bozo doesn't believe his friend so they decide to go to one of the local hangouts with a bunch of guys to do a scientific experiment. The bozo bets $20 he can intimidate these supposedly unflappable eastern chicks. So, he unzips his fly, let's it hang out and strolls across the crowded bar to a bunch of these eastern ladies followed by his buddies. When he gets to the girls, he points to his peter and says, "Excuse me ladies, do You know what this is?" One of the girls peers down to where he's pointing and says without hesitation," 'It looks like a penis only smaller.'" The guy was so deflated, he just hung his head and walked away, another hapless victim of some sharp tongued eastern women."

Chuck laughed." Okay coach, I believe you now. I'll make sure I don't go into any New Jersey bars without an extensive in-country briefing from either you, Marco or Freddy."

"However, in spite of this enlightening discussion of the regional differences of the opposite sex, we can't spend any extra time in your fair city to test the theory. Although I'm one of the world's greatest dalliers, we can't dally here. We have to be off to Dallas after your little tour tomorrow," Tony said.

"This guy is unbelievable Chuck. Maybe you can talk some sense into him. First he gets me into this whole dumb match and now he's so obsessed with the whole thing that we have to drive across half the country before he'll admit how ridiculous this scheme really is," Marco said in disgust.

"I don't know Marco. You know I rarely agree with Tony and his cockamamie schemes. He's gotten me into trouble too many times. But, from what he's told me, you have an obligation to publicly humiliate this asshole. Or you could just kick the crap out of him in the town square at high noon," Chuck said.

"I can't believe you guys. I thought sure you would talk some sense into Tony, Chuck. That's why I agreed to come down here. You've always been the logical, levelheaded one in our group. I was sure you'd put an end to this, but you're just like these other bozos. How does Tony cast a spell so easily over so many otherwise intelligent people," Marco said in exasperation.

"Because he's correct in this deal," Chuck said seriously." That's why I never tell anyone I was in Vietnam anymore. I got tired of getting debated by all of the turkeys who want to analyze and reanalyze why we there. They refused to believe that for us it was very simple. We were in the army, we went where the duly elected government sent us. We served our country under very difficult circumstances. We came home and now we just want to be left alone. However, you can't just say that to these turkeys. So, I got tired of playing their games. Besides, I also got tired of duking it out every time I went to a bar. It's not a good deal for a struggling lawyer to be in fist fights three times a week. However, once they raise the issue, all of us need to respond. You have a chance to publicly respond. There are a lot of New Jersey guys you don't even know who need you to win this," Chuck said seriously.

"This guy's great. You must be a hell of a lawyer Chuck," Tony said slapping him on the back. "I've been trying to tell our little buddy that for a week. You did it far more eloquently in two minutes."

"What a bullshitter. I'm glad to see that age hasn't dimmed your capacity to pass out crap," Chuck answered with a smile." Helen," Chuck yelled to the passing waitress," my friends and I will have four brews. And tell Scotty to be extra generous because these are some old Army buddies of mine."

"Be right back Chuck," the waitress said as she threaded her way through the crowd to the bar.

"Scotty's a good guy. He was with the First Cav in 1968. He's the only guy in here I can talk to about the war." Chuck said.

The waitress returned quickly with a tray full of beers. "Here we go boys," Helen said as she set two beers in front of each man. "And Scotty wanted me to give you this," she said as she handed Chuck a folded napkin.

Chuck unfolded the napkin, smiled and showed the other men that the bartender had written 'Welcome Home' in big letters. They all smiled and turned to the bartender raising their beers in salute.

Scotty saw them and smiled broadly and gave them the thumbs up sign. They all turned back to each other, touched their glasses and said in unison, "Welcome Home."

* * * *

It was still dark in the apartment when Chuck woke them with his imitation of a reveille bugle call."Ba pa pa, Ba pa pa, Time to rise and shine," Chuck yelled.

"What time is it?" Marco asked sleepily." We just went to bed."

"It's five o'clock private," Tony said as he rolled off the bed and pulled the covers off Marco. "Today is a big day for us and we need to get an early start. Chuck let us sleep an fifteen extra minutes because he said this neighborhood is secure enough so we don't need a mad minute to clear the area."

"Yeah, there's nothing like having a whole battalion firing weapons when you first wake up. That even used to wake Marco up instantly," Chuck added.

"Were you guys always strange or did the army do that to you?" Marco asked." If it was the army, you should be able to collect about 90% disability, because I estimate you only have about 10% of your brains still functioning."

"Well, lucky for you I'm going along with you so now you'll have 20% brain power guiding your tennis career my 10% and your 10%," Chuck said with a smile.

"All right," Tony said excitedly." So you're going with us?"

"Yep, I kind of made contingency plans when you called me. When I saw you guys last night, I knew I had to go on this mission. I have to make a few more phone calls this morning and then we're on our way to creating the new John McEnroe," Chuck replied.

"Way to go Chuck," Tony added as the two men embraced and then jumped on Marco sleepily sitting on the side of the bed.

"Assholes," Marco managed to say before being smothered with pillows.

* * * *

"Pull over here Tony," Chuck instructed." It's only a block away from here." The bantering had died down as the men sensed they were approaching their destination. They got out of the car and

followed Chuck in silence as he led the way. A cold mist had settled on the ground making visibility difficult. The dampness and
ominous gray clouds of the early-morning seemed to cast a solemn
pall on the whole scene. Chuck, who was several steps ahead of the
others, approached a clearing in the trees. Through the trees, Marco
could see the black granite wall. He instinctively slowed down and
then hesitated. For some reason, seeing the long wall caused him
to remember the first casualties he had seen in Vietnam. His company had moved up to support a Vietnamese unit that had been
ambushed. By the time they reached the ambush site, the VC had
fled leaving behind about 20 dead Vietnamese soldiers. The dead
had been placed in a pile, awaiting evacuation to a morgue.

Marco had first seen the corpses from a distance of about 50
yards. He remembered that he had forced himself to go closer to the
pile of bodies to see how he would react. Then, as now, he hesitated.
Then, as now, he forced himself to move forward because he was
a soldier. He thought it ironic that in both cases, twenty five years
apart it was the dead, the refuse of war, that had caused him to act
the same way. Then it was the bodies of Vietnamese soldiers piled in
the hot sun. Now it was the black granite wall, a symbol of the death
of his own countrymen.

Marco paused at the end of the clearing and studied the wall.
He had always known that over 52,000 servicemen had been killed
in Vietnam. But, to see all of their names displayed on such a long
monument, filled him with sadness soon followed by a feeling of bitterness at the loss of lives that the wall represented. He could feel
his throat constrict and his eyes well up with tears. He knew it was
partially out of anger at the futility of the sacrifices made by those

whose names were inscribed on the wall. He also felt a deep sorrow, an aching sorrow that seemed to fill his entire body.

In spite of the sadness that the wall evoked, Marco felt drawn to it. He moved slowly closer to the monument, wanting to touch it but dreading being able to read the names. As he approached the wall, he noticed that the others had already reached it. As he read the names neatly arranged, guilt mixed with his sorrow. Somehow we felt guilty that he had come home and those on the wall had not, as if there were some supreme lottery that had whimsically selected these 52,000 and not him. He felt the sorrow and anguish this wall represented. He thought of the countless mothers whose worst fears had been realized.

And he thought of the numerous children who never got to know their dads or granddads. He wondered why he had been allowed to come home. In one almost unbearable moment, he could feel the sorrow well up in him and overwhelm him. His eyes filled with tears and his throat tightened so much that it hurt. But he couldn't cry." *God how I wish I could cry,"* he thought to himself. *"I feel so sad for these guys and yet I can't cry. Why can't I cry?"*

Finally, when he couldn't stand it any longer, he retreated to the edge of the clearing to wait for his companions. One by one, they joined him. He had no idea how long they were at the wall. "Let's go," Tony said solemnly when they were all together again. They walked slowly and silently back to the car. It had started to rain more heavily, but none of the men seemed to notice.

CHAPTER NINE

TERRY

The van strained and wheezed as it ascended the winding unpaved road. Marco shifted into low gear as the grade became steeper. Loose rocks and gravel on the roadway spun away as the tires sought to gain traction on the shifting surface. "This would be a great place for an OP if the fields of fire were a little cleared out," Marco said as he struggled to hold the jerking steering wheel steady.

"I believe you underestimate the skills of the former recon platoon leader Marco. If you'll look closely, which you never do, you'll see that the underbrush has been altered quite cleverly and just enough to give Terry a clear view of anyone coming up this road. And the sound of the gravel and rocks under the tires is enough to alert him long before we get to him. My guess is he's even now making sure his shotgun or rifle is within easy reach," Tony said.

"You know I think you're right." Chuck added. "Add some concertina and sandbags and this place would remind me of a few places we visited during our all expense paid trip to exotic Southeast Asia."

"Yeah, maybe. But, the pine trees need to be replaced by some triple canopy then we'd have a real Deja Vu. Although I don't know who wants that kind of Deja Vu," Freddie spoke loudly from the back seat to be heard over the sound of the rocks and gravel popping and pinging as the vehicle made its way up the road.

The fading afternoon sun, filtered further by an ominous overcast sky made visibility difficult. The jerking headlights of the van poked erratically through the gloom as the vehicle fought its way to the top of the hill, barely visible in the fading sunlight.

"I hope Dr. Dracula is at home," Chuck said peering intently at the landscape which took on an eerie look as the shadows danced away from the vehicle. "It'll be a shame to come all this way without seeing the old coot and not giving him a chance to judge who has the best looking neck arteries."

"You're right my friend. This does look like the start of a bad Bela Lugosi movie," Tony added with a smirk. "Marco needs all his blood for the match as do I as the brains of the outfit. However, you two bozos have more than you need. As a matter of fact Fred, as I recall you have several pints of borrowed blood you got at the MASH after you sought out that grenade in Viet Nam. It's time you gave the blood back anyhow."

"Now wait Tony. Let's not talk about who borrowed what." Chuck leaned forward to be heard. "After your little escapade in that ambush, I have it on good authority that you have hardly any original parts left in your body."

"And you Marco," Chuck started out playfully......

"Shut up Chuck," Marco's angry command shattered the jovial mood in the car.

After an awkward moment of silence, Chuck said quietly, "Yeah, OK Marco. I understand."

After a short pause Marco said softly. "I'm sorry Chuck. This whole trip has me a little on edge."

No one else said another word until they reached the summit of the hill. Through the fading light the men could see the outline of a rough log cabin. A lantern from within weakly illuminated the front porch. They could see their friend Terry sitting in what appeared to be a home-made rocking chair, a rifle across his knees.

"Can I help you gents," he yelled out as they pulled up in front of the cabin. His question was more of a challenge than an offer of help.

Marco brought the van to an abrupt halt.

"Oh crap. I bet he has a sign and counter sign, and we don't know it," Tony feigned fear. He opened the door and stepped in front of the headlights where Terry could see him clearly, his hands in the air. "Don't shoot Terry, it's Tony and your other old Buds from the 1st of the 14th. We don't know the sign and counter sign. We're here because the S-4 sent us to tell you that when you turned over your platoon in 1967 you were missing a canteen. Just give us the eight dollars and forty cents and we'll be on our way."

Terry studied him for a moment without any change of expression. After a moment, a slight smile crossed his face. "No need for a sign or counter sign. I would recognize your bull shit a mile away Tony." He slowly removed the rifle and leaned it carefully against the wall of the cabin and made his way down the stairs.

Tony met him half way and embraced him. "Boy, it's good to see you again Terry. When we parted in '67 I wasn't sure I'd ever see you again."

By then the others in the vehicle emerged and embraced Terry in turn, each grateful to escape the tense mood that had overtaken them after Marco's surprising outburst.

"C'mon in. I don't have much, but I believe I can find a few beers for you," Terry led the way into the cabin grabbing his rifle as he passed it.

"It's not much." Terry said as he led them into the dimly lit cabin.

"Ah, I see that you're still the master of the understatement," Tony answered. "Why, my hooch in Pleiku was the Ritz compared to this."

"I've seen abandoned crack houses that were nicer than this," Chuck added as they all laughed.

They all stood near the doorway and observed the interior of Terry's living quarters. The cabin was indeed austere. They could see an army cot with a sleeping bag in a corner near the large stone fireplace. An old, battered sofa sat by itself in the other corner. Several rifles and shotguns were arrayed on pegs along the walls. A small card table stood in the middle of the single room surrounded by one folding chair and several wooden crates. A few dirty tin dishes were piled on the table.

"It's not much," Terry repeated as he cleared off the dishes and placed them in a sink the men hadn't noticed initially in a darkened corner. "However, it's got everything I need," he said unapologetically as he fetched another lantern.

When lit, the second lantern brightened the interior of the cabin considerably. It also seemed to brighten the mood of the men who had been shocked initially by seeing Terry's primitive living conditions.

"You know Pal," Chuck said as he sat down on the sofa, "if this is what floats your boat, you should go for it. I can almost see the attraction of wanting to live like our ancestors did 300 years ago," Chuck added sticking his finger in his mouth while pretending he was gagging.

"I know it's not for everyone, but it gives me the privacy I need except for when assholes from my distant past show up unexpectedly to ruin the mood," Terry said with a smirk.

"Marco, Chuck, go out to the van and get the provisions we brought, before we completely lose the mood the recon platoon leader has described so eloquently," Tony ordered.

Marco and Chuck left the cabin and returned shortly with three cases of beer and several boxes of groceries.

"OK boys, even though I know our host was ready to put out a marvelous spread, let's show him that we are not without couth and refinement when visiting others even if their level of couthness does not match our own," Tony said as he unloaded the boxes. "It's an international feast, pepperoni and cheese from Italy, Vienna sausages from Austria and crackers from wherever crackers come from. Bring that dining room table over here Marco, I feel like dining in front of the fireplace."

"Ah, our leader Tony is always ready, like the artillery, to add dignity to what otherwise would be a simple and crude gathering," Chuck said while distributing the beers.

"Well too bad you boys brought your own food and drink, I was about ready to break out some vintage American cuisine, C-rations of the WWII variety which was provided to us in Vietnam from a grateful nation," Terry now seemed more relaxed as he went to a cupboard near the sink. "Ah yes, it's still here. The piéce de résistance, the creme de la creme of C-rations, Ham and Lima beans."

All of the men made a gagging sound simultaneously and then laughed.

"You know Princess Di had a wonderful humanitarian project to remove unexploded mines and other ordnance from Southeast Asia. I always thought I owed it to the people of Vietnam to go back over there and help to dig up all of the cans of Ham and Lima beans that GIs buried in their beautiful country. There's got to be a special place in hell for the guy in Natick who thought that Ham and Lima beans was a combo that would appeal to hungry, growing young American men," Chuck joked.

"Nah it was not some guy in the quartermaster that thought it up, I'll bet it was someone's Aunt Edna who knew what American fighting men needed. I'll bet you she hated the lack of nutrition in the doughnuts that the Doughnut Dollies served us," Tony laughed.

"Well, reminiscing about the cuisine of our screwed up war is certainly one way to spend a pleasant evening with old friends," Terry pronounced while dragging the folding chair to the table. "However, I hope you have a more rational reason for coming all this way to find me."

"What makes you think we weren't just driving across the great state of Pennsylvania and decided to check out Hooterville? It does kind of have an alluring sounding name," Tony said as he opened a can of Vienna sausages.

"First off, it's Hobsonville. Second, nothing you do is haphazard. You try to make everything you do seem unplanned, but I know better. I'm even betting you stopped off at my house and my wife told you where to find me. It's obvious to me that you've already put in considerable time to arrange this 'unplanned, spontaneous' meeting. Plus, it can't be an accident that you've gathered up some of your 'Merry Men' to partake in whatever nefarious scheme you are plotting." Terry took a long swig of his beer and sat back.

Tony moved to the edge of the sofa. Out of the corner of his eye he noticed Marco perched on a wooden crate, his arms folded across his chest. He looked at Terry for a long moment before he spoke. "You always were the perceptive one of the group Terry. You can read people a mile away. That's why we need you in my, uh ...our nefarious plot."

Terry just stared at him. No one else spoke.

"You were always the one that asked the hard questions, without regard for the consequences or worrying about whose ox might get gored. You're the best truth seeker I know. It's a skill we can use on this mission." Tony paused for a moment, looking down at his hands. "I remember the first operation that our new Battalion C.O. conducted. Colonel Miller had just left us for a new assignment in Saigon. We all loved that guy. He had trained us in Hawaii and was with us when we deployed and for our first six months in country. Then in comes Colonel Cooper, a certified REMF, looking to get his ticket punched and pick up a medal or two at the same time."

"That would have been a tough gig for anyone, replacing the Chief Dragon half way through our tour," Terry interrupted.

"Kind of you to acknowledge that now Terry. I remember you weren't so understanding and sympathetic that day he swooped in on us to launch his first operation," Tony said cooly while popping a small sausage into his mouth.

* * * *

They all looked up as the helicopter circled and began its descent into the LZ. Shirtless GIs , enjoying the warm sun, lounged around the interior of the open area, sleeping or eating their canned meals. In the tree line bordering the landing area, other soldiers could be detected in full combat gear hunkered down in their fighting positions keeping a wary eye on the wooded area beyond the perimeter. The dust and wind kicked up by the chopper as it settled onto the landing area loosened several of the poncho shelters that had been erected nearby. Disgusted soldiers ran to retrieve articles being blown away by the close proximity of the helicopter.

"Tony warned us that the new Battalion C.O. would be coming this afternoon. That's probably him. I better go greet him, " Terry said rising from his seat on a wooden ammunition crate. "Sergeant Foster, alert the squad leaders that we may be going on an operation soon. My guess is the new guy will want to flex his muscles as soon as he can to show that he's now in charge," he yelled over his shoulder as he made his way to the helicopter now beginning to shut down in the center of the LZ.

"Yes sir, wilco," the sergeant yelled after him.

Terry recognized Tony, the HHC Company Commander, Major Stevens, the Battalion Operations Officer and Captain Jackson, the Artillery Liaison Officer as they disembarked. A fourth officer, a Lieutenant Colonel, strode briskly toward him. His starched uniform and new jungle boots set him apart from the other three whose rumpled uniforms and worn boots gave evidence of their long use and many washings.

Tony tried to keep up with the fast moving new Battalion Commander. "Terry, this is........he began before being interrupted.

"I'm Colonel Cooper, the new C.O. You must be Ryan the Recon Platoon Leader."

"Yes sir. Happy to meet you. Come this way to my CP," Terry said as he led the group to his command post, a poncho liner tied to a few trees for shelter from the sun. "Goodrich, get us a few more ammo crates," Terry ordered a nearby soldier when they arrived at his crude headquarters.

In a short time they all were seated on the makeshift chairs. The Colonel looked around first at Terry's CP then let his gaze sweep the activity in the LZ without saying a word.

"The recon platoon got in just last night from a five day patrol Colonel," Tony broke the silence.

"I'm aware of that Captain," Cooper said curtly while continuing to scan the platoon's position.

"What's your disposition here Lieutenant?"

"We're on 75% stand down sir. One quarter of my men are manning dug in positions in the tree line around the perimeter or in OPs further out."

"Do you think that's the right balance, given that you're out here by yourself?" The Colonel asked pointedly.

"Yes sir. I wouldn't do it if I didn't think it was right, " Terry said looking straight at the Colonel. Terry's jaw was set, an almost imperceptible red hue showed at his neck line. "The men had a tough five days in the boonies and need some time to recover. I can't get them recharged if I have them all on perimeter duty," Terry added.

The Colonel sat back on the ammo crate and crossed his arms on his chest, looking at Terry more closely.

"We don't have much prep time for the operation. I believe we should get on with the briefing," Major Stevens broke the awkward silence.

The Colonel continued to stare at Terry for another moment before he spoke. "OK let's get on with it."

"Terry, we're going to conduct a battalion sized search and destroy operation in this area," Major Stevens said while spreading a map out on the makeshift table. "We'll launch from three LZs. You'll be picked up here at 0700 tomorrow and be lifted to LZ Sleepy located here," he said pointing to a point on the map. "Alpha and Bravo companies will be picked up at the LZs indicated which they are moving to right now. They'll be dropped in the areas shown, LZs Dopey and Sneezy. Charlie company will move overland and be prepared to support whoever becomes engaged. I'll leave an overlay of the operation with you so that you can transfer it to your own map. I'll have the complete Op Order to you no later than 1400 today."

Terry's jaw tightened visibly as he viewed the map. His thin lips became an almost imperceptible line in his weather beaten, tanned face as he continued to study the map. When he finally spoke his voice had a slight edge to it. "Major Stevens, Colonel, with your permission, I'd like to point out a few problems I see with this plan," Terry said looking at each officer in turn.

"Go ahead Lieutenant," the Colonel said cooly. "I'm interested in knowing where the S-3 and I may have erred."

Terry stiffened and straightened up. He looked at the Colonel for a moment before he spoke. "First, my platoon needs a resupply of ammo and rations. Many of my men are in need of new uniforms and boots. They got pretty beaten up in the boonies. The S-4 already told me we would be resupplied by tomorrow. Second….."

"Have the S-4 get his ass in gear and get this platoon resupplied with whatever they need this afternoon," the Colonel commanded Major Stevens.

"Second," Terry continued, ignoring the interruption still looking at the Colonel. "With all of this activity, the bad guys will be alerted. We haven't been in this area for long so we don't know what strength the enemy might have here. Each of the LZs you've selected are too far from each other to be mutually supporting. If one of us gets into a tough fight we're on our own. Charlie company coming overland won't be able to help any of us until late in the day. And lastly and most importantly, we'll be outside the range of our direct support artillery if we move that far in a single jump." Terry sat back without removing his gaze from the Battalion Commander.

"Is that true Captain Jackson," the Colonel turned to the artillery representative.

"Yes sir, we discussed this earlier and I told you we can move a 105 battery to support you by 1600 tomorrow. They can't be ready before that," he answered. "If you could postpone the operation 48 hours, we'll be in position to support you."

"Captain, I told you earlier this is a war not a golf match that can be rescheduled. I told the General that we would kick off at 0700 tomorrow and by God that's what we're going to do. Major, move the four deuce mortar platoon into a supporting position that will cover as much of the Area of Operation as possible. If the artillery won't do it we'll do it with our own organic indirect fire support."

Everyone stared at the Colonel for a moment before Major Stevens, the Operations Officer, spoke up. "Sir, we shouldn't put the four deuce platoon out by itself without some additional security. I'm going to have to task one of the line companies to give us a rifle platoon for security for the mortars."

"No goddammit, I want a maximum effort devoted to the search and destroy operation. Can't anyone in this sorry battalion follow orders," the Colonel yelled. "Just make it work Major Stevens or I'll find someone who can. Is that clear?"

For a moment the group was stunned by the Colonel's outburst. Major Stevens was the first to speak. "Yes sir, it's clear. He then turned to Tony and said in a calm, measured voice, "Tony you're going to have to scrape up some additional troops from the headquarters company to provide security for Harry's four deuce platoon."

"Yes sir. I'll do it and let you know what I've done," Tony answered.

"Terry, I'll have the location of Harry's platoon noted on the overlay with the appropriate firing fans. We'll try to position him to provide maximum support to you and the line companies. The first thirty hours will be critical until we can get the artillery into position. Be aware of that as you move on the first day. Harry is good, but his ability to conduct multiple fire missions is limited."

Captain Jackson spoke up. "I'll find out if there are some general support 155s or 8 inch assets that might be in range and might be available until we can get you the direct support you should have. They'll still have their general support missions, but I should get us on the list for that first day. It'll also be a little tricky for your assigned Forward Observers because the commo to the big guys is a little different."

"Great Dan. Let me know if you find something. If you do, I'll need the procedures and radio frequencies for the artillery addendum. I believe that should cover it. Anyone have any questions," Major Stevens concluded the meeting without looking at the Colonel.

The group was silent. No one moved. "Sir we have a lot to do. We better get back to the battalion CP. There's a lot of coordination that needs to get done in the short time we have before we kick off," Major Stevens spoke up.

Everyone looked at the Colonel who was once again studying Terry. "Tell me Lieutenant" he said sarcastically, "how does a First Lieutenant get so smart about battalion operations that he feels qualified to question his battalion commander's plan."

Terry stared back at the C.O. and without hesitation replied, "Well, spending seven months in the boonies has certainly helped, but beyond that I couldn't tell you Colonel."

The Colonel stood up. Everyone followed. "Being smart, as in smart ass isn't always good Lieutenant," he said as he turned and made his way back to the waiting helicopter followed by the other officers.

"Roger that sir," Terry said cheerily after them.

Tony lingered with Terry as they both walked slowly behind the others. "That was as close to insubordination as I've ever seen in this man's Army," Tony said as soon as they were out of earshot.

"Fuck him. What's he going to do, send me to Vietnam?" They both laughed. "Soon as my time is up, I'm getting out anyhow. Look around you. See those thirty six guys in this LZ. That's why I put up with the bullshit. They need me and I need them. I'm going to protect them as much as I can from that tin horn, REMF colonel who doesn't know a good operation from his ass. Colonel Miller spoiled us. He taught us to speak up and contribute. He listened and then made up his mind. When he finally came up with his plan we were all on board. What you saw today was the exact opposite of that. This op has all the characteristics of a totally screwed up goat rodeo. I can smell it coming"

"Captain DeJulio get your ass on board or we'll leave you here," the colonel yelled over the whine of the chopper's rotors as it got ready to depart.

"See you Terry, take care of yourself," Tony yelled as he ran to the helicopter.

* * * *

"Yeah, I remember that day clearly. I knew it wouldn't turn out well and it didn't. The new Battalion C.O. was a rookie and it showed all over him and that damn operation he cooked up. No one could talk him out of it. I know the S-3 and the rest of you tried, but he was determined to get into the war as soon as he could," Terry took a swig of his beer before continuing.

"However, I believe he was just starting to catch on to becoming a good C.O. when he died in that helicopter crash several months later."

"Yeah, I believe we should give the old guy the benefit of the doubt. I met up with Major Stevens, our old S-3 at a 25th Infantry Division reunion several years ago. He said that Colonel Cooper was really rattled by how badly that first operation turned out. He became much more receptive to listening to everyone's input before making his own decision," Tony added.

"It's only too bad that we had to lose some very good people while he was commanding during his training wheels phase," Terry said looking down at the rough, wooden floor of the cabin.

There was silence for a moment before Terry spoke up cheerily, breaking the mood. "But, I'm sure you gents didn't come all this way just to reminisce about the bad old days and the foibles of the human character of Lieutenant Colonels. No siree, I'm willing to bet that crazy Tony has conned you malleable youngsters into going on one of his half baked, absurd adventures. I further believe, looking at the assemblage of this motley crew he's recruited, that it has something to do with the unfortunate experience we all shared back in 1967," Terry carefully set his beer on a nearby crate and sat back, folding his arms across his chest.

Tony was the first to speak. "Not so, Buffalo breath," he said with a smile. "Yes, I admit to being a little unconventional sometimes, but never crazy. And our adventure, as you call it has all the elements of being a noble enterprise. Its objective is to publicly humiliate an effete, pretentious draft dodger who impugned all of our honor and service. Plus, there's a girl involved. And there's one thing more which you can't understand because you're not Sicilian - vengeance."

Before Tony could continue, Terry said emphatically, "Count me out." His smile faded. His eyes blazed and at the same time his face darkened in contrast as he moved to the front edge of his chair. "I'm out," he said louder this time. "You can go on your silly crusade Tony, you always were one to tilt at windmills and mythical monsters. I want to bury that sorry assed part of my life. I was a soldier and I did what the duly elected government asked me to do. It wasn't fun for me to go. I was newly married and my wife was pregnant. But that's what soldiers do. I saw a lot of good people get hurt and die," his voice was rising now.

"And when I got home, what did the country do after I gave up a year of my life?" the words were coming faster now. "They shit on me that's what they did. They accused me of killing babies and innocent people. They worried more about those weak kneed ass holes that went to Canada and Sweden than they did about the GIs they had sent to fight a difficult war."

He paused for a moment before he spoke in a softer voice, "But, Tony I'm way past that now. I don't give a rat's ass what the civilian population thinks about our involvement in the war. As a matter of fact, I don't want any recognition or sympathy from anyone. I just want to be left alone with my own memories. I only care about what you guys and the other Vietnam vets think." He sat back again, perspiration visible on his face.

"But you don't even know what we're going to do," Tony said. "It'll be a good chance......

"No Tony," Terry screamed, "I don't want any part of it. I shoveled that shit into a hole a long time ago. I don't want to dig it up again and the country certainly doesn't want to revisit it either. Leave it alone Tony. And if you can't do that, then please leave me alone...... please," Terry said almost in a whisper as he got up and moved to the sink.

The group sat silently for a moment, stunned by Terry's passionate outburst.

After a moment, Chuck spoke up, "OK Terry, OK. We know how you feel. We were just hoping," he said hesitatingly, "we were all just hoping that as part of this trip we could all spend some time together. I know now that's not possible. We all certainly can respect your view."

"Yeah, we get it Bud," Marco added. "As a matter of fact we probably have over stayed our welcome a little. It's time we got going and let you get back to whatever it is you do here," he said with a smile. "Plus, we have a long drive ahead of us tonight."

They all stood up. Tony walked over and put his arm around Terry. "We love you Bud. We'll miss you on the trip, but we understand. Now that we know where your hideout is, we'll come back to visit you again."

Each man walked over and hugged Terry then quietly left the cabin. Terry followed them to the front door and stood silently observing them while they all got in the van. As they pulled away, they could see that he rendered a perfect salute. He held the salute until they were out of sight.

No one spoke as Marco slowly guided the van back down the narrow gravel road. Darkness now made the drive back down the hill more treacherous then it had been earlier. The only sound was the pinging of the rocks in the roadway. The headlights searched the darkness as Marco negotiated the twists and turns of their return route. The wooded hillside gave the impression that there were fleeting shadows darting among the trees while barely revealing the narrow roadway between the trees. The only sound heard in the van was the crunching of the rocks disturbed by the progress of the van as it made its way slowly down the mountain. When they finally reached the junction with the paved road at the bottom of the hill, Marco stopped the van and turned to Tony." I think Terry is right. This whole idea is stupid. We're going to make fools of ourselves and in the process we'll just dredge up a lot of the controversy that has finally receded. He's right. It was a bad deal. It's time to let it go Tony"

Tony sat totally still, staring straight ahead. Finally, a single car passed on the road ahead of them. In the light of the vehicle's headlights, Marco could see Tony's face. His jaw was set, his eyes fixed on some unseen distant object.

"I agree with Marco, Tony. Nobody wants to hear from a bunch of has-been soldiers. Why don't we just scratch the whole tennis match thing and turn this into a road trip with our buds," Chuck said quietly from the back seat.

For a long time Tony continued to stare into the darkness. Finally, without turning his head he hit the dashboard with his fist." No God dammit! I'm not running anymore. And I won't let you guys run either." He half turned so that he could face Marco and those in the back." I'm tired of running." His voice was rising. "It's time we act like we feel. We did a tough job that many of our fellow citizens wouldn't or couldn't do. I'm proud of that and you should be too. Every time we let some blowhard like Barrington get away with ridiculing our service we give him legitimacy. I respect Terry, but he's dead wrong. It's time to take a stand. I'm not running anymore and I won't let you guys run either." He turned away staring straight ahead again" No more," he said softly."No more."

Marco stared silently at Tony for a long moment before glancing at his companions in the back seat. Without saying a word he eased the van on to the paved road and resumed the journey.

They drove in silence for several hours. The gloomy western sky in front of them seemed to reflect the mood in the vehicle. Tony was the first to speak after they went through the first toll booth in Ohio. "You know what boys? I'll bet I could make this trip blindfolded and I'd be able to tell you when we enter and leave every state along the way," Tony mused. Without waiting for a response from anyone, Tony continued." I know you're all very interested, so I'll tell you how I can do that. As you leave New Jersey, the toll takers get pissed off and yell at you if you don't have the exact change or you don't have your money ready. In Pennsylvania, they take your money, but don't say anything. In Ohio, they take your money and thank you. As you enter Indiana, the toll collectors thank you and tell you to have a nice day.

Marco smiled in the darkness. He knew that Tony's soliloquy was an attempt to lighten the mood and relieve the tensions of the last few hours. He was grateful for the effort. Tony always seemed to be able to defuse tense situations with just the right humor at the right time. He also admired Tony's unique ability to convert his own observations or even the smallest aspects of life into some philosophical conclusion that always amused Marco. He always seemed to extract some monumental humorous lesson out of events that most other people didn't seem to notice.

"Tony, you're so full of bullshit, I'm surprised you haven't already drowned in it, " Freddie said to a chorus of laughter from the others in the van.

The bantering continued for several more hours as the van rolled westward across the flat Ohio landscape. At around midnight, silence again pervaded the vehicle as the occupants fell asleep, one by one.

CHAPTER TEN

BOB

Tony pulled the van to the side of the road and stopped. The sound of the tires crunching on the gravel and the sudden halt awoke the sleeping passengers.

"We're here," Tony announced unceremoniously.

"No, this can't be it. There's nothing here."

"Yeah, that's right Chuck, you slept for the last 600 miles and you know I'm wrong. This is it. Trust me this is it. Bob said the intersection of County Road 6 and Haymarket Road and that's where we are. This is where he said he'd meet us."

The finality of Tony's statement suppressed any remaining objections contemplated by the others. The joking and good-natured kidding had evaporated much earlier during the long, cramped, ride across the endless midwestern prairie.

Without another word everyone got out of the van, anxious to distance themselves from each other and the vehicle which now seemed to be the repository of the ugly mood which had descended on the group.

Tony moved away from the others into the cornfield bordering the road. The cold wind felt good on his face after so many hours in the heated van The wind carried with it the threat of the harsh weather that would soon descend on the Midwest. In another month this wind would take away a man's breath on this unprotected open area. The field which still held the stubble of the corn crop harvested earlier, had the look of a disheveled and unshaven giant. The turbulent November sky seemed to mirror Tony's mood. There was constant movement above the horizon, as vague dark gray and black shapes fought each other for control of the pre dawn skyline.

Tony's feet sunk into the moist, black soil as he walked. He felt the mud curl over the edges of his shined shoes. Feeling the earth and seeing the sky always made him feel better. Ever since his Army days, Tony had developed a confidence that he could survive and even make himself comfortable in any kind of environment. It was a source of pride for him that he aggressively challenged the environment, no matter how harsh it was. As he walked, he unzipped his jacket wanting to feel more of the cold wind on his body.

The other men moved away from the van, stretching and joking with one another. Tony moved further from the group, scanning the barren horizon searching for any indication of Bob's arrival.

The wind lessened as the sun began to slowly brighten the eastern skyline. It reminded Tony of Ranger School after all night patrols when it seemed always to get warmer just before dawn.

Breaking dawn in Southeast Asia was so different from those in the U.S., Tony thought. In Vietnam, he remembered, the dawn broke suddenly, bringing daylight quickly to the Central Highlands. He was always grateful for the rapid transition from nighttime to full sunshine, bringing relief from the night long vigil of ambush patrols. However, in Vietnam the daylight made no promises about the dangers that might lie ahead in the hours to come.

Dawn in the U.S. is more gentle, heralding more placid events for the coming day. The sun's arrival, he remembered from his many night long patrols in Ranger school, was more gradual. It almost seemed that the sun was reticent and had to be slowly coaxed to perform its daily routine of lighting the eastern sky.

Dawn in both places however, was preceded by a silent calm as if the earth was gathering its strength and preparing itself for another day of human activity. In the stillness, Tony scanned the horizon listening intently for some activity or sign that Bob was coming.

Not a sound disturbed the silent dawn except for the low murmur of his friends gathered around the van several hundred yards away. Finally, Tony heard a barely audible drone off in the distance. He told his friends to be quiet, trying to identify the source of the sound as he moved quickly back toward them.

Everyone now eagerly searched the skyline seeking the source of the hum disturbing the quiet morning. The unknown noise grew louder before Marco yelled," There it is, it's a plane," pointing into the gray sky.

"False alarm, it's a plane not the car we were expecting" Chuck announced as he resumed his observation of the distant roads and fields.

As the plane got closer, Tony said triumphantly," Not so fast Gorgonzola breath. Remember that the B Company commander is the master of the unexpected. He knows we're watching for him to arrive by land. My bet is he won't do that."

"Look, someone threw a package from the plane," Marco said excitedly.

After observing the object dropped from the aircraft, Tony jokingly said," That's no package. That's an out of shape, overweight former paratrooper. My guess is that it's our former lean warrior comrade who has succumbed to twenty years of creature comforts."

A parachute blossomed over the object, slowing its descent." It's him, it's him." The men yelled in unison as they jumped up-and-down embracing one another.

The jumper skillfully steered the parachute toward the men and then landed with a thud in the soft dirt of the field, thirty yards from the group.

They all ran laughing and joking to their friend while he struggled to free himself from the parachute harness. Tony grabbed Bob while Chuck, Marco and Freddie ran further into the field to push down the now billowing parachute canopy which had been partially reinflated by the increasing morning wind.

"My compliments on a truly dramatic arrival Bob, but we can't give you many style points for that awful PLF you showed us when you landed," Tony said as he held on to to his friend." I've seen air dropped jeeps land more softly than that," he said laughing and clapping Bob on the back.

"How the hell are you?" Tony walked arm in arm with Bob now that he was freed from the parachute."I told these guys to expect the unexpected from you and you didn't disappoint me."

"I knew that you would anticipate my surprise Tony. I wanted to trick you by coming in by submarine, but that's hard to do in the middle of Indiana," Bob laughed.

"Well, let me have the boys gather up your chute and other gear and load up the van. Let's get into town and find some hot chow and a gallon of coffee so we can talk talk over old times," Tony started to lead Bob to the van.

"Oh no, or as you would say,' not so fast Gorgonzola breath' I'm not letting you and your chubby friends revert back to the soft and easy life you've grown accustomed to. No sir, we're going to spend a pleasant day and night in the field just like the old days. Well, not exactly like the old days. No one will be trying to kill us out here," Bob gestured to the open field.

"Oh no, I'm not going to spend any more time sleeping in that cramped van. I've had all I can take sleeping in close quarters with a bunch of snoring, farting, cranky old men. My days of roughing it are over."

"Who said anything about roughing it my unimaginative friend? Are you insinuating that we Hoosiers are incapable of providing you with a refined field experience? Are you impugning the abilities of Amy's Catering and Party Service to arrange a rustic experience that will impress even you effete, eastern snobs? I ask you to withhold judgment until after Amy and her staff have completed their version of roughing it," Bob said as he scanned the horizon.

"Ah-ha, I spy Amy's caravan approaching us from the east, even as you doubters question the veracity of my words," Bob pointed off in the distance where two vans and a pickup truck were stirring up a column of dust as they approached the group.

Just short of the men, the small convoy turned on to a road bordering the cornfield where they stood.

"Let's wander over and see if Amy and her crew can match the magic that our mess sergeant was able to produce with just a few marmite cans," Bob yelled over his shoulder as he followed the vehicles down the dirt road.

The men soon caught up to the convoy which had halted in a clearing. A number of people were scurrying around unloading the vehicles and setting up tents and tables.

"Mess Sergeant Amy doesn't full around," Tony said as he watched the organization and rapidity with which the campsite was being prepared.

While the men looked on, the catering crew rapidly set up a grill and eating area with chairs, a table and a small canopy. The table was quickly set with plates, utensils and linen napkins.

"If you gentlemen will sit down, we'll take your orders for breakfast," an attractive young woman said as she directed them to the dining area with a sweeping gesture.

"The ever efficient and gracious Amy invites you bozos to enjoy some Midwestern hospitality which will by far exceed your own uncouth, eastern bozoness," Bob said as he led the men to the table.

"In spite of our host's less than eloquent introduction of us, I assure you that we as his guests are grateful to be under your charming and expert care," Tony said as he bowed deeply before the woman.

"Amy, this is Tony, the rascal I warned you about," Bob said as he put his arm around Tony." Keep your apron on at all times and count the silverware after this gig is over," he said with a chuckle.

"Ah that Bob, even though he is so inarticulate it's clear to see that he is such an incurable romantic," Tony extended his hand to Amy." We are just grateful his parole officer allowed him to come", Tony said as he punched Bob in the arm.

The smell of cooking bacon and brewing coffee, quickly wafted over the impromptu picnic area.

"Well now that the introductions are completed we're ready to start serving," Amy said as she moved toward the table and the waiting men. We have sausage, bacon, eggs any style or omelettes to order. We also have at Bob's request, chipped beef on toast, or SOS, although why you call it SOS is beyond me."

"Because if we called it CBOT, people might confuse it with the Chicago Board of Trade," Tony quickly responded as the group erupted in loud hoops and hollers.

In a short period of time, Amy's crew served the men a prodigious amount of food. Another group of her team set up pop-up tents with air mattresses and sleeping bags in an adjacent area.

By now the sun had risen higher in the sky, taking the chill off the morning air. "I don't know about you guys, but I can hear that sleeping bag over there calling my name," Chuck said as he patted his full stomach." What's the schedule Bob? Will we be here for a while?"

"Yup, We'll be here overnight. Amy's crew will be back for a steak cookout later on. There are sandwiches and beer in those coolers over there. For those of you who want to stand down, those tents around the perimeter contain all of the creature comforts you need for a good siesta," pointing out the now completely assembled tents.

"I'm up for that," Marco said."Spending all night trying to sleep in a cramped seat with four sweating, snoring men is not conducive to getting a good night's sleep. I'm with Chuck," he said as he followed his friend.

Gradually the others followed. The campsite became quiet except for the noise of the catering crew cleaning up.

* * * *

"Well, that's just what we needed," Chuck said as he joined the others around the fire. I didn't realize how tired I was. I believe this little respite is exactly what we needed before our final push to Dallas."

"I'm with you Chuck," Tony said as he poked a log in the fire pit."I can't believe I slept seven hours. Even Marco's usual snoring didn't bother me."

The chill in the air returned as the sun settled low in the western sky. The cloud cover obscured the remaining sunlight, bringing a rapid end to the day." You got the LPs ready to go Bob? We don't want anyone to sneak up on us and steal any of Amy's steaks that I smell grilling," Tony pointed to the catering crew's preparation.

"Not to worry big boy. There's no one within several hundred miles of here brave enough to get between us combat hardened vets and that choice meat over there," Bob said.

By the time the steaks were served, darkness had set in. A small generator hummed steadily near the catering truck, providing light for the evening cleanup. "We're all cleaned up and ready to go Mr. Murphy. Is there anything else we can get for you before we leave?" The catering manager asked.

"No Larry, you and your crew did an outstanding job. Convey our gratitude and undying love to your boss Amy on another successful party. You provided an experience these eastern snobs don't deserve and won't soon forget. The only time they saw Indiana before today was from 30,000 feet. I believe after today they'll have a new appreciation for Hoosier hospitality thanks to you and your crew," Bob rose and shook hands with the manager.

Each of the men rose from their place around the fire and shook hands with the departing crew.

"We'll be back before dawn to prepare your breakfast," the manager yelled back as he led his crew to their truck.

The men settled down once more around the fire, bundled up against the chill wind which had returned with the darkness. "Distribute those beers Marco," Tony said "It's time to kick back and recall the golden years when we were young soldiers."

"Here we go again. Let's everybody wallow around in the worst year of our lives," Marco said as he handed beers to those around the fire.

"Ah ha what a cynic you've become my friend. Yeah, in many ways it was a bad year. But, in many ways it was the best year of our lives. We forged unbreakable bonds with some of the finest people America produced including those now burping and farting around this campfire. Whether you care to acknowledge it or not Marco, we've been blessed with friendships that most people don't get to experience. And, my cynical friend, we have those strong ties precisely because we made those friendships under very adverse conditions, conditions you continue to describe as our crap year," Tony pointed his beer at Marco.

"Ah, the old Italian philosopher waxes eloquently and yet truthfully. We share friendships deeper than most other people ever experience," Bob added.

"And I think between the beer you're drinking now and all the cordite you whiffed in Vietnam coupled with the sounds and concussions you experienced over there, your brains got scrambled. You can pretend it was just a tough class trip, but you'll never convince me that it was anything other than a crap year where a lot of good people got hurt and killed. So my dear friends, I'll not be a part of your delusional recollections. I'm off to bed. I hope the beers dull your senses enough so that the stories you tell sound believable," Marco turned and moved swiftly to his tent.

The men all looked after him as he entered the tent."It's better this way," Tony said softly. "It will give us a chance to talk openly about what really happened on November 19. We couldn't do that with Marco here. Any talk about that day pushes him to the edge."

"Well, we have most of the key players right here. It's as good a chance as we'll ever have to reconstruct what happened," Chuck said."We all have a piece of the story, but no one except Marco has the whole story. I was wounded and medevaced out right after my company got ambushed. I have a good recollection of what happened until then."

"And I got lifted in to replace you, so I know what happened on the ground after that until I got wounded. I was also monitoring the Battalion net before that so I have a pretty good idea of what went on between you guys and Colonel Cooper," Tony said as he took a sip of his beer.

The group was silent before Freddie spoke up." That operation was screwed up from the moment it began."

* * * *

"Andrews, where the hell are those choppers? They were supposed to be here 45 minutes ago."

"Sir, they're still socked in by the fog at Pleiku. The aviation commander believes based on the weather forecast they'll be able to launch in 2 to 3 hours," The S3 Air answered.

Colonel Cooper slammed his hand on the small wooden table that served as his desk." God dammit they committed to be here at 0700. They're already an hour overdue and they haven't even left yet. They're 45 minutes away. I told the general we'd begin the operation at 0700.

"Sir, the general is at Pleiku. He can see the fog and most certainly would understand the effect the weather is having on the aviation unit," Captain Andrews explained in a measured tone.

"God dammit captain. Don't you understand anything about command? The general isn't looking for excuses. He wants his commanders to show initiative when obstacles arise," the Colonel rose and glared at the young staff officer.

"Sir, actually this delay isn't all bad. It will mean less time that we'll be without our direct support artillery. And C company has already started their overland move, so they'll be closer to the LZ's of the lifted companies and will be better able to support them if anything happens."

"Major Stevens you're the God damn S-3. It's your job to anticipate and plan for contingencies like this so that the battalion meets its mission commitments. You don't get paid to accommodate adversity by putting a happy face on it," the Colonel's screaming carried beyond the CP tent.

Major Stevens took a deep breath to control his own emotions." Sir, this whole operation has been designed to tightly coordinate all components of the battalion. If we start tinkering with parts of it now, it'll have an adverse impact on every other part of it."

"Doesn't anyone in this sorry battalion understand the importance of mission commitment?" Colonel Cooper yelled." We could be here all day if those pussy aviators decide the weather isn't to their liking. So, here's what we'll do. I want A and B companies to start humping overland. When we get word that the choppers are getting ready to launch, we'll direct the companies to some interim LZ's. Major Stevens I want you do a map recon and choose some potential LZ's along each company's route. We'll launch this operation by phase lines. As each company hits a phase line, that will trigger a new LZ.

Major Stevens stared at the Colonel not believing what he was hearing." Sir, I believe if we just have a little patience for a few hours…."

"God dammit Major you execute my order as I've just given it to you or I'll relieve you on the spot. Is that clear Major?" Colonel Cooper moved closer to his S-3 pointing a finger in his face.

"Yes sir, it's clear." Major Stevens said as he saluted and moved quickly to the TOC to amend the operation order.

The hour following the battalion commander's outburst was chaotic. Both A and B companies who had been ready to move to the LZ and were organized by stick for a helicopter lift, were now directed to begin an overland move immediately. Major Stevens contacted the aviation company and other support units to alert them to the change while his staff changed the written order.

Colonel Cooper moved throughout the landing zone goading everyone to speed up their preparations. When he finally returned to his command post, he summoned his radio operator. " Jones, get Brigade on the radio," he ordered.

"Pioneer six is on the horn sir," his RTO announced after a minute.

"Pioneer six this is Dragon Six. Operation Bluebell has launched, over," Colonel Cooper announced. There was a self satisfied smile on his face as he transmitted the message.

"Roger that, out," a voice answered.

The exchange was brief as both parties wanted to minimize any chance the enemy might intercept the message.

The next few hours became even more confusing. When the fog lifted and the helicopters were ready to launch, they received orders to shutdown and wait until A and B companies could reach the first LZ's along their overland routes.

* * * *

Chuck poked a log in the fire. Without looking up he said," It was a goat rodeo. We were receiving radio messages from Cooper every 15 minutes wanting to know our location and telling us to move more quickly. I could hear him on the Battalion net pushing Marco also. Then, when the fog lifted at Pleiku, things got even worse. He got a command and control helicopter and was flying all over the place first over Marco, then me, then C company and the recon platoon. He was like an angry hornet, crisscrossing the sky from one end of our operating area to the other. If the bad guys didn't know we were up to something before he got his chopper, they sure knew it once he started his airborne imitation of the road runner."

* * * *

"Dragon 16, get a move on. You're still five clicks from your LZ. The choppers are now ready to launch and are waiting for you to get there so they can pick you up," the Colonel repeated his message of 15 minutes earlier."Let me know when your lead elements arrive at the LZ. Out"

"If that SOB had kept his pants on for a few hours we'd be loading up at the LZ right now the way we were supposed to," Sergeant Cole said disgustedly." Instead, we're still an hour and a half from linking up with the choppers. If he had been involved in the D-Day invasion of France we'd still be in boats in the English Channel."

"Well Seregeant Cole there's nothing we can do about it now. We just have to suck it up and make this new plan work the best we can," Marco said as he adjusted his pack while maintaining his place behind his lead platoon.

"Dragon One Six, this is Dragon Six over," the radio crackled again.

"Don't answer it sir. He'll think we're having reception problems. The troops are starting to get spooked by all this useless commotion he's making. He's like a fart in a frying pan up there, flitting across the sky every 10 minutes, pointing out our location to every bad guy within 20 miles."

"Dragon One Six, this is Dragon Six come in, over," the voice was more insistent.

"Let me have that handset Golinski," Sergeant Cole ordered the RTO while taking the hand set from him." This is… moving through… dense… reception… will notify… out," this sergeant released The push to talk button after each short phrase, transmitting a fragmented message to the battalion commander.

"Dragon 16 say again. Your message was garbled," the voice seemed more frantic.

"Golinski, periodically push the 'push to talk' button and give him a shot of squelch to convince him we're trying to communicate. The captain needs a break from being henpecked so we can concentrate on moving the company and planning the next part of this dumb operation," Sergeant Cole instructed.

Marco smiled to himself pretending he didn't hear what was going on behind him. His company struggled through the underbrush under a constant barrage of messages from the battalion commander aloft. He tried to ignore the incessant goading of his superior and focused instead on the security requirements he needed to follow as he moved deeper into what he knew was enemy territory.

The colonel became so frustrated by Marco's progress that he once landed in a small clearing along the company's route.

Marco couldn't believe the battalion commander would so blatantly reveal the exact location of his company's position by landing amidst the column of men.

The Colonel leapt from the helicopter before the skids touched the ground and sprinted toward Marco." Captain Covello, you're way behind the other units. You better get your ass moving or you're going to screw up this whole operation," he yelled over the sound of the helicopter idling a short distance away." If you can't get the lead out of this unit, I'll find someone who can."

Marco could tell the troops around him were watching and listening closely to the meeting between the two officers. He felt a weariness come over him which he had kept at bay until now by the adrenaline driven activities of the last 18 hours. He looked past the Colonel at his troops who had automatically taken up the defensive positions they always assumed when stopped. When he looked back at the Battalion Commander there was anger in his eyes." Colonel you do what you have to do. However, until you make a change, that's what I'm going to do. I'm going to make sure my company moves as quickly and securely as it can to accomplish the mission." He pulled his pack higher on his back, cradled his rifle and resumed his march.

Sergeant Cole, standing nearby witnessed the exchange. He glared for a moment at the Colonel before following his company commander, shouting to his men," Okay boys let's move out. Maintain your distances and keep alert, especially on the flanks."

The column came to life again and resumed the march. Colonel Cooper remained stationary as the men moved silently past him. As the end of the formation reached him, he realized that he and his helicopter would soon be alone in the clearing. He quickly moved back to the chopper and ordered the pilot to lift off.

* * * *

Chuck sat back and looked at the now totally dark sky. A beer rested precariously on his chest. "Well, we finally linked up with the choppers in those en route LZ's, four hours after we would have launched if Colonel Cooper had kept his pants on. What a goat rodeo. Nothing went the way we planned it once he changed the original timetable."

Bob stared into the fire. The reflection of the flames in his eyes seem to highlight the intensity on his face." All the unnecessary commotion and activity must have alerted every bad guy within 50 miles of us. We couldn't have helped them anymore unless we dropped leaflets with the op order in it all over our area of operations," he said grimly.

"Yeah they seemed to know exactly what we were up to," Tony stood up." I was monitoring the battalion net and I could tell by all the contact reports that they seemed to know where all of our units were."

Tony paused, looking off into the now darkened cornfield."-Except Marco," he said softly."Except Marco's company. They had no contact. We figured out later that they were slowing you guys down but letting Marco walk into the trap."

"We had a hell of a time making any progress once we left the LZ where the choppers dropped us," Chuck stood and pushed a log back into the fire with his boot." There were snipers all along our route. When we tried to flank them, we ran into more snipers and dug in positions. By the messages we heard on the battalion net we could also tell that C company and the recon platoon were being slowed down the same way. I got hit when I tried to maneuver one of my platoons against one of the prepared positions.

"When I heard you were down, I decided to get involved," Tony said.

* * * *

Tony thought he could hear the thump thump thump of an in bound helicopter. The late afternoon sun had disappeared behind the western mountains, making visibility difficult." Shhhhh," he admonished those around him as he strained to hear the distant sound.

"There it is," Someone pointed to a speck in the sky approaching rapidly from the southwest.

"There are supposed to be five wounded on this first chopper," Tony announced." You got enough people to handle that doc?" He said as he turned to the senior medic in the group.

"Affirmative sir. There'll be more people here shortly to meet the other Dust Offs that are following," the medic answered.

As soon as the helicopter landed, teams of stretcher bearers rushed to it and quickly unloaded the wounded soldiers. Tony watched grimly as the medical crew efficiently tended to the broken and wounded bodies now in their care. He moved closer to the pilot's window." Where's Captain Murphy?" He yelled over the whine of the helicopter's engine.

"If you mean the company commander of the bunch we just brought in, he's back at the LZ waiting to be medevaced on our next trip. He told us to load his men first and come back for him," the pilot answered.

"How soon are you going back out for him?"

"Just as soon as we refuel, about 20 minutes."

"Good. I'm going back out with you. I just have to get my weapon and a few other things. I'll see you at the fueling point," Tony yelled over his shoulder as he ran back to his hooch.

Tony grabbed his equipment and rifle and loaded it into the jeep which was waiting for him outside his tent. As soon as he climbed in, the vehicle raced to the refueling point. He jumped aboard the helicopter just as the crew chief was releasing the main rotor from its tie-down. As the pilot increased the power, the machine began to whine and tremble slightly as if it was anxious to rejoin the battle.

After a forty-five minute flight the chopper set down in an area that had been hastily cleared by the waiting troops. It was barely large enough to accommodate the single helicopter. Tony hopped off before the copter had landed and began searching the faces of the wounded men lined up on the ground. The dust, fading light and bandages made it difficult for Tony to find Bob quickly. He grabbed a medic who was racing toward the helicopter."Where is Captain Murphy?" He yelled over the din in the clearing.

"Over there by that tree," the medic pointed to a small clump of trees at the edge of the clearing. "He'll go out with the next load. He wants all of the other wounded to go first," the medic said as he moved quickly to the helicopter.

Tony move rapidly in the direction the aid man had pointed. He kept his eye on the bandaged figure propped against a tree. He knew even from a distance it was his friend Bob Murphy. He couldn't get over how small and fragile his friend looked. As he got closer he could see blood oozing through the bandage on Bob's chest. Bob smiled weakly when he saw Tony, his white teeth a stark contrast to his dirty face which now held a gray pallor.

"Uh-oh. The battalion must be in bad shape if they're sending the Headquarters C.O. out to the field," Bob reached out for Tony's hand.

Tony gripped his friend's hand tightly."I couldn't let you guys have all the fun. Besides when we get back to the world, I'll now be able to inject some truth into your otherwise fantastic stories."

Tony could feel Bob's grip tighten as he coughed." Smart of Cooper to send you out to replace me."

"Who said anything about Cooper. I came on my own. Don't tell him I'm here," Tony paused and studied his friend more closely. He could see the pain in Bob's eyes." You've got a million dollar wound Bob, but you need some medical attention. I'm sending you back on this chopper."

"Oh no you're not. My men go first," Bob tried to push himself up but fell back. His breathing became more labored.

"I'm the company commander now. I decide who goes when. You're out of here," Tony said with finality while signaling a medic." Captain Murphy goes on this chopper. Get him loaded."

The medic and several soldiers put Bob on a stretcher and moved him quickly to the waiting helicopter. Tony watch the chopper lift off with his friend and the other wounded soldiers, then moved quickly toward the sound of the battle. Once clear of the tiny

LZ, he picked his way carefully through the brush, stopping periodically behind a tree to try to determine the disposition of the embattled company.

The troops were strung out along a narrow trail, with some squads trying to maneuver to the flanks. Tony moved cautiously forward by darting from tree to tree, pausing at each location to try to make sense of what was happening.

"There are snipers in those trees ahead sir. That's what's holding us up," a soldier said as Tony dropped down beside him.

"Who's in charge now?" Tony asked.

"Lieutenant Reynolds. He's up ahead with the command group by that little clump of trees just to the right of that big anthill," the soldier pointed forward without raising his head." Captain Murphy was wounded and taken to the rear," he added.

"I know, I saw him. He's on a chopper on his way back to the hospital right now," Tony said as he peered through the smoke and brush to his front. He studied the terrain ahead for a moment then dashed to a tree near the giant ant hill he could see about thirty yards in front of him.

As he lay panting at the base of the tree, he tried once again to make sense of the firing that raged around him. The soldiers he could see were hunkered down, searching for targets. Periodically, they would expose themselves briefly and fire bursts to their front. It seemed to Tony that the company's defensive fires were sporadic and not very effective. Off to his right he was able to make out the small command group, about twenty yards away. Once he caught their attention, he told them through hand signals that he would join them. They acknowledged that they understood and then pointed to the tops of the trees to warn Tony of the snipers that had them pinned down.

Tony nodded. He got on all fours behind the tree then jumped up and sprinted to the group. A bullet thunked into a tree behind him as he crossed the open area. He fell down heavily among the men of the command group.

"Lieutenant Reynolds," he said after he caught his breath, "what's the status?"

"We got snookered sir. They let part of the column get by them then they sprung their ambush. The company is strung out from just in front of us back to the small clearing you probably came in on. If we only had artillery support we could get some defensive fires in here and bring the company on line," the lieutenant said.

"The artillery should be up soon," Tony answered."What was the last ready time you got from them?"

"Anytime now. Lieutenant Johnson, our FO, says they're in place now. They've been overloaded with fire missions from the minute they got it established. Everyone needs them. C company and the recon platoon had priority because they ran into some heavy shit first," Reynolds pointed to the forward observer with this back to a tree speaking into a radio.

At that moment, the FO turned his head to Tony and Lieutenant Reynolds. He smiled and gave a thumbs up."On the way, wait," he yelled to them. In a short time, they all heard the locomotive sound of artillery overhead followed by the crump of exploding rounds in front of their position.

"See if you can give us some fuse quick rounds in those trees to our front. Maybe we can shake some of the snipers out of their nests," Tony yelled to the FO.

"Wilco sir," the FO answered then spoke into the radio. Within minutes artillery rounds were crashing into the treetops to their front. Using hand signals, Lieutenant Reynolds directed the platoons to come online to bring more firepower to bear on the enemy in front of them.

Feeling more confident with the artillery support, Tony. peeked around the tree to assess the situation. As he peered into the trees in front of him, he detected movement. He caught sight of a sniper just as he leveled his rifle in Tony's direction. Tony moved instinctively back to the protection of the tree. He was too slow. The sniper's bullet entered the top of his right shoulder. Because he was prone, the round traveled the length of his upper body and exited just above his waist.

He was still conscious, but he knew he was badly wounded. Lieutenant Reynolds who had heard the bullet slam into Tony's body, quickly pulled him completely behind the tree to protect him from any further wounds.

Tony began to drift in and out of consciousness. He could tell someone was applying a battle dressing to his wound to slow down the bleeding. Through the fog above him he could make out someone saying as it from a distance," Comfortable… pain… morphine."

* * * *

When Tony regained consciousness he was in the MASH back at Pleiku. The whole right side of his body ached. Every time he moved his right arm, there was a sharp pain along his back. When he was able to focus his vision he stared into the beautiful blue eyes of an attractive young woman. "Well, if I died and you're the attending angel, this won't be all bad," he smiled weakly.

"Wow. Even after an operation and being heavily sedated, you grunts can still focus on the charm offensive. I can tell already that you'll be making a quick recovery, Captain..." the woman paused as she read his chart,"Captain DeJulio. I am Justine O'Reilly. I'm helping out in this ward since we have so many casualties."

"How lucky for me," he said. "Don't let the food stains on my uniform or my unshaven look fool you. Once we grunts get a chance to clean up we can be as charming as anyone else."

Tony suddenly felt very tired. As he closed his eyes, he could hear Justine say,"I'll be back to check on you." Tony smiled as he drifted back to sleep.

* * * *

"What a lucky SOB you were Tony. I don't know how you did it, but to get that Justine to take a liking to you was quite an accomplishment. Even after you were repaired and the sympathy should've worn off, she stayed with you," Chuck said as he sipped his beer.

"She was one great woman," Tony said without looking up." She's the reason I worked so hard on the docs to let me stay at the MASH to recover instead of letting them ship me out to another hospital. She's also the reason those last few months in Vietnam helped to cancel out some of the not so great memories I have about that year," Tony said wistfully.

"Oh my God! Tony has managed to turn our time together from thrilling war stories to a sappy soap opera," Bob stood up and stretched his back.

"Do I detect some jealousy being expressed? While you bozos were trying to charm Montagnard princesses, I got to spend time with an all-American girl," Tony said as he threw a twig at Bob.

"Wait a minute. Before you boys wander off to the land of make-believe, I think we should continue the narrative. I for one would like to finally know all the pieces of that day. We now know the story of the company from Bob and Tony. How about you Chuck?"

Chuck got up slowly from his chair, leaning on a long branch he had fashioned into a walking stick earlier in the day. He rested his chin on the stick as he stared into the fire." They sucked us in," he said finally.

He used the stick to rearrange the logs until the embers glowed like bright red rubies at his feet. The grim set of his face was clearly visible to everyone by the light of the re-stoked flames." They really sucked us in," he sighed."We were moving rapidly, trying to get into position as quickly as possible to support which ever of the airlifted companies needed us. He paused for a minute then poked the fire again, this time more violently." The recon platoon, which was in the lead flushed out several NVA. We thought we had surprised them, but it was all part of their plan. The NVA soldiers took off. The recon troops dropped two, but several more got away. That got the lead troopers of the recon platoon excited and they ran after them. Terry tried to stop them, but they were like bloodhounds who finally saw the rabbit that had been teasing them after a long chase. That and the constant prodding and badgering from Colonel Cooper in his

C and C helicopter above us overwhelmed our normal good sense and caution.

"Not a day goes by that I don't think about that precise moment, when the column changed from an orderly movement to a ragged chase. The recon platoon took after the NVA and my company took after the recon platoon. By the time I was starting to rein them in, the bad guys had sprung their trap."

Chuck looked off into the darkness as if he could see someone or something in the distance. He stared for a long time before he looked back at his friends who were watching him from around the fire. "They were in the trees and in prepared positions all around us," he said softly." The recon platoon was pinned down to our front along with my lead platoon. It took me a while to bring my other two platoons on line because of the snipers. We finally got them out of the trees and linked up with the recon platoon late in the afternoon after we were able to get some artillery support. By then, the rest of the battalion was in trouble and we were in no position to help."

Chuck sat back down in his chair with a heavy sigh. He seemed to be exhausted by his recollection of the events of almost thirty years earlier. When he spoke, it was with some bitterness." Not a very heroic turn of events," he said as he sipped a beer.

"I know how you feel pal," Tony said after a momentary silence." We all have basically the same story. That piss poor battalion plan had us screwed from the moment it started. I know we all have 1,000, woulda, coulda, shouldas from that day. But the truth is that we had a bad plan and the bad guys took advantage of every weakness that Colonel Cooper baked into the operation.

Tony stared into the fire for a moment before he jumped up." You know what?", he said as he moved around the fire slapping each of his friends on the back."You know what? This is the first time since it happened that we all have had a chance to tell our piece and put the whole story together. I think it was good, at least for me, to finally talk about that awful day. I never discussed it with anyone before and I doubt if I will ever do it again. That's why you guys are so important to me. We shared some shit days like that one, but we also shared some good days. There are not many guys that have the memories we have nor share the bonds those memories gave us. Pick up your beers boys while I propose a toast," Tony was more upbeat now. He waited until all of his friends stood and raised their beer cans. "Here's to the crap war we had. It was the only one we had and we did the best we could with it. It did one very good thing. It brought us together and that's worth an awful lot to me."

"Here, here," they all shouted enthusiastically.

When they all took their seats again, Chuck looked at his friends seated around the fire." There's only one thing missing from your toast Tony."

"Oh yeah and what's that?" Tony answered.

"We don't have Marco's piece to the story. And, to a large degree, we don't really have Marco in the brotherhood."

Tony stared into the fire for a long moment. When he looked up, the flames reflecting off his eyes made them seem as if they were ablaze. His jaw was set, making his mouth look like a tight line across his face." You're right Chuck. That little shit has kept his story and all of his emotions about that day buried deep inside that scrawny little body of his. I was hoping that this trip with you boys would have allowed some of his long suppressed feelings to leak out. I was also hoping that by goading him and forcing him to confront the WASP king, I could put him back in touch with the passionate and 'never say die' guy he once was."

"Well, based on what I've seen so far on this trip, I don't believe you're going to see any leaking or get any clues about what happened to Marco on that day or any other secrets he has trapped in his Italian noggin," Bob said.

Tony jumped up and pointed a finger at Bob." Not so fast Gorgonzola breath. No one knows my paisan better than I. It may not look like anything is happening to defrost him, but I see some tiny signs that the volcano may corrupt sometime in the not too distant future. I don't expect you emotionless Northern European Neanderthals to be able to discern the subtle changes in our little buddy. But, I as a direct heir to the great erudite and sensitive philosophers of ancient Rome and the Italian Renaissance ......

"And Mussolini," Chuck yelled out.

Tony paused and stared at Chuck for a moment and then continued." As heir to the great Roman and Italian philosophers, I'm telling you that it may look to you as though nothing is happening, but I can assure you that Vesuvius is stirring." Tony put his hands on his hips and look defiantly at his comrades.

They remained silent for a moment before they pelted him with sticks and any other objects that were handy." Here's what we think of you Cicero," Chuck yelled.

When the rain of objects ceased, Tony smiled and said," That last immature outburst proves my point." That brought on a renewed onslaught of more thrown objects and a loud chorus of boos.

Tony held up his hand." Alright, alright. Just to be sure of my position, I have an ace up my sleeve. I know that Sergeant Cole, Marco's Feld First, lives in west Texas, about three hours from Dallas. I have an appointment with him while we're in Dallas. He'll be able to tell us what went down in Marco's company that fateful day."

"Aha. Finally, the philosopher king of bullshit and keen student of human nature reveals his secret. He asks people who were there what happened. What a concept. Why couldn't we Neanderthals think of that," Bob said before he threw another stick at Tony.

"Speaking of Dallas, we're taking off from here tomorrow at zero dark 30. That's real early for you guys who never understood army slang. I'll be around to roust you before dawn, so pack up your things tonight. Amy and her crew will be here around midmorning to break down the camp. Now get some sleep. We have a long day of driving tomorrow. Dallas here we come."

CHAPTER ELEVEN

TOMMY

"Okay you guys, wake up. we're approaching downtown Dallas," Tony said excitedly.

"What time is it Tony?" Bob asked sleepily.

"Almost 8 o'clock," Tony answered." We hit this just right. I think every beautiful girl in Dallas is going to work right now."

They all sat up quickly, stretching to undo the stiffness from their all-night ride in the van. Pal you're right, this is unbelievable. You hit H-hour right on the nose," Chuck said.

"Let's get a closer look," Tony said as he eased out of traffic and pulled slowly to the curb." Okay you guys, coming up on the right is one of the finest sights in Texas," Tony said seriously.

He drove the car very slowly behind three attractive women walking together on the crowded sidewalk. Tony followed them for a few minutes until they noticed the car. Other drivers began to noisily indicate their impatience with the slow moving vehicle.

"Tony I think we ought to buzz off before we tie up all of the traffic in Dallas," Marco said.

"Yeah I think Marco's right," Chuck added." It looks like you slowed down a whole lot of folks Tony."

"Okay, even though I think I'm in love, I'll get us out of here. But, let's leave them with the military courtesy they deserve. Let's give them one of those famous 1st of the 14th eyes right," Tony said with a grin." And let's make it crisp. Everybody sit up."

All of the men sat up straight as Tony pulled the car even with the women who had now quickened their pace." Ready, eyes right," Tony boomed out the command.

Tony and Chuck sitting on the left side of the vehicle, snapped their heads to the right. Marco and Bob on the right side and Freddy in the middle, stared straight ahead. All had a very somber look on their faces. The girls began to laugh while continuing to walk. Other pedestrians stared at the slow moving vehicle with its ramrod straight occupants. Tony kept his position for about a minute, watching out of the corner of his eye for busses which pulled in and out of the curb lane.

"Ready front," Tony commanded, as both he and Chuck snapped at their heads to the front. As they did so, Tony put on his directional and eased back into traffic. In the rear view mirror, Tony saw one of the girls throw a kiss." Oh my God, look up, they're in love too," Tony exclaimed." We have to go back. One of them just threw a kiss."

"I think the joke is over Tony, and I am sure the drivers of Dallas are grateful. Besides, if you screw around much longer, we'll be late in meeting Tom. And that would be just like you, Tony. You have to drive all night to get here and then screw it up in the last half hour," Marco lectured.

"Yeah, you're right again Marco," Tony said." Even though it was a short but intense love affair, I think I'll get over it. As a matter of fact, I think I see someone else up ahead who could help me to forget her."

"Uh-oh Tony, you'd better be on your best behavior because there's a cop following you," Freddie cautioned." Too late. He's got his lights on. He wants you to pull over Tony."

"Oh crap. Don't these guys know that we're just trying to have a little fun," Tony complained.

"I'm sure it's just a little misunderstanding. As soon as you tell him you were trying to have fun instead of disrupt the traffic flow of the city of Dallas, I'm sure he'll send you on your way," Chuck said sarcastically. "I'm sure once he sees our Yankee license plates he's going to know immediately what a kidder you are. And you know how amused southern cops can be with a car load of fun loving Yankees."

Tony once again pulled the car to the curb, this time stopping. The patrol car pulled in behind them." Now don't you guys screw this up, let me handle it. I'll get us out of this."

"This is great. He ties up all of the traffic in the heart of downtown Dallas and he doesn't want us to screw it up," Marco said."I would also like to remind you guys that this is the same guy who convinced you that you should follow him here to Texas on this cockamamie scheme. Doesn't that give you a warm feeling about your decisions to give up two weeks of your lives."

"Maybe I should show him a little leg, Tony? Do you think that would encourage him to go easy on us?" Bob chuckled.

"Nah, I think that would only work in San Francisco," Tony answered.

Tony, Chuck, Freddie and Bob were trying to control their laughter when the policeman approached their vehicle. Marco sat somberly, obviously not as amused as his comrades.

"You guys look like you're having a good time," The officer said with mock amusement." I guess you think it's pretty funny to inconvenience all these folks while you play your stupid games."

"We didn't mean any harm officer," Tony said seriously not wanting to antagonize the policemen any further.

"Well maybe up in New Joisey," the policeman caustically mispronounced the state," this is good clean fun. Down here, we have more respect for other folks, especially our women. Let me see your license and registration," he ordered.

The five men sat quietly while the officer examined the documents Tony produced. Pedestrians slowed down and peered into the vehicle adding to their growing discomfort.

"Who are you guys?" The policeman barked as he stuck his head inside the vehicle.

Each of the men answered in turn with his name.

"What's your business in Dallas?" The policeman asked Tony sternly.

"We're here in Dallas to pick up an old army buddy we haven't seen in 25 years," Tony said hoping the army buddy part would evoke some sympathy from the officer."These guys are all old Army buddies. We're kind of having a reunion," Tony added hopefully.

"Get out and open the back of the vehicle," the policeman ordered, apparently unimpressed by the reunion story.

Tony got out of the van and walked to the rear of the vehicle, accompanied by the policeman.

"Marco turn the rear view mirror so you can see and let us know what's happening," Chuck whispered.

Marco quickly repositioned the mirror so that he could see the two men behind the van." They stepped away after looking in the back so I really can't see what's going on," Marco reported.

"I hope being neat doesn't count with the Dallas Police Department, because Tony packed the van like he used to pack his duffel bag," Bob chuckled, his humor returning.

"Yeah, if this guy is Felix Unger, Tony is in big trouble. I know he'd rather get a ticket then have to repack the van neatly," Chuck laughed.

Just then, the back doors of the van slammed shut. Marco could see the two men engaged in conversation."They're talking now. I can't believe it. The cop is laughing. I think Tony's weaved his spell on this guy also. I just can't believe it. I wouldn't be surprised if he talks the guy into leaving his squad car and going with us on this dumb trip," Marco groaned."Tony makes the Pied Piper seem like a failure."

They all turned in time to see Tony and the policeman shake hands. Tony returned to the car with a scowl on his face while the officer returned to his own vehicle." That prick," Tony said as he got into the vehicle.

"We didn't have room for him in the van anyhow Tony," Chuck said smiling.

Tony started the car and again eased out into traffic." That prick," he said again." He was in the Cav the same year we were in Vietnam. When I found that out I was sure he'd let me off the hook. But the prick gave me a ticket. Hell, he spent some time in the Ia Drang Valley. He walked on the same ground we were on. And he was a grunt. I would have expected that from a REMF, but not a grunt. That prick," Tony said with finality.

"Let me see that ticket Tony. Maybe we can just mail the money in and we won't have to get hassled by any appearance," Chuck said.

Tony passed the folded yellow document back to Chuck without a word."Well, I'll be…," Chuck exclaimed, showing the ticket to Bob. In large letters the policeman had written only two words, 'Welcome Home'.

* * * *

"There he is. He didn't grow up at all in 20 years. How many 42 your old guys in this country are sitting on their duffel bags on their front lawns," Tony said.

Yeah, why can't he be as mature as we are, doing adult things like driving across the country for no good reason," Marco said seriously.

"We are continuing to ignore you Marco. Largely because if we listen to you we might kick the shit out of you and that might make it harder for you to play good tennis," Tony answered.

"Okay you guys, let's pretend we don't see Tommy. He doesn't know my car so I'll drive by him. Let's all look across the street and point when we go past him," Tony instructed.

They were past Tommy before he recognized them. All of the occupants were looking in the opposite direction while Tommy was yelling and waving. Tony shot a look at the rearview mirror and could see their friend running after the van, trying to signal the occupants.

"Oh what a sad sight. Even I feel bad. Poor Tommy really thinks we missed him," Tony said. "We'll swing around the block and beat him back to his house."

When they came down Tommy's street again, they could see him in the distance, walking back to his house slowly with his head down and his hands in his pockets. Tony stopped the car and all four men piled out of the van and ran up to the front door ignoring Tommy who was now running back up the street. The four men pretended to be knocking on the door when Tommy called to them breathlessly. As if on cue, they all turned, ran down the steps and jumped on their friend, wrestling him to the ground.

"You guys are as stupid today as you were 25 years ago," Tommy said from the bottom of the pile." I was so afraid you guys might have become adults in the intervening years. Thank God, assholes never change. Let's go inside. Claire made breakfast. Actually, we were expecting you guys about an hour ago, so it may be a little cold by now," Tommy explained.

"Well, we would have been here on time, but Marco insisted on screwing around a little," Tony said with a grin." You remember how he always used to get us into trouble. Well, he hasn't changed."

"Somehow, I don't remember it that way Tony. And I am sure I'm not getting the right story now, am I guys?" Tommy said putting his arm around Marco.

"Baby, these are the guys I've been telling you about," Tommy said to the attractive woman who met them at the door.

"So this is Claire. You look just like your pictures of 25 years ago. We always envied Tommy because of all the letters you sent to him over in Vietnam. You kind of were a link for all of us to the states because you wrote so regularly and so eloquently. You were great then and you're certainly great in person," Chuck said as he kissed the woman on the cheek.

"Welcome home," Claire said as she hugged each one in turn. She then lead them into the dining room where a small feast of biscuits, rolls, ham and bacon were laid out." Sit down and I'll bring the grits while Tommy takes your egg orders," Claire said.

" You know they had a 25th division Reunion here a few months ago," Tommy said as he finished his meal." There were a lot of World War II and Korean war guys, but there were also a good number of Vietnam vets there. As a matter of fact, I met a guy from your company Marco. He lives over in Fort Worth. His name is Hudson. He really thought a lot of you. Poor guy lost part of a leg in that big fight you guys were in. But he really gets around well. He's a stockbroker for Dean Witter, doing real well. Maybe we should go by and see him."

"No. I don't want to see him now Tommy," Marco said emphatically.

"Well, maybe we could call him. I know he'd like to talk to you," Tommy persisted.

"Tommy I'm sorry. I just don't want to talk to him," Marco said curtly."Excuse me, where's your bathroom?"

Clair led Marco from the room, leaving the other men to stare silently after him, somewhat surprised by his intense response to Tommy.

"Marco has had a lot on his mind lately," Tony explained quietly.

* * * *

They stood for a moment in the tiny entrance to the bar. Off to their left they could see two bartenders scurrying around serving a number of patrons sitting and standing along a bar which extended the entire length of the wall. The rest of the pub had a number of tables crowded in the center of the room, while spacious booths lined the perimeter.

Tony slowly scanned the crowded room before he saw a small, unoccupied table in the center." Follow me," He said as he made his way through the congested floor. There were only three chairs at the table." We need two more chairs," Tony announced.

"Chairs!" Chuck yelled over the din of the noisy crowd. People in the immediate vicinity looked at him, puzzled by his outburst.

"Hey dickhead, what are you doing?" Bob asked quietly." These people think you're nuts."

"Tony wants two more chairs, so I'm getting them. Chairs!" He yelled again.

"Sit down and be quiet. Come on Marco let's find some chairs before this bozo gets us thrown out of here," Bob said as he and Marco moved quickly to find two unoccupied chairs.

Tony smirked and slapped Chuck on the shoulder." That's the kind of response I like when I issue commands," he said.

When they were all settled at the table, Tony studied the crowd more closely.

"Uh-oh. I don't like this. Tony is looking for targets of opportunity." Tommy said watching his friend closely." Please Tony, no scenes. I have to still live here after you leave."

Tony paid no attention to him as he scanned the room. Suddenly he stopped. His eyes narrowed, a smirk played across his face." Oh my God. It's the Holy Grail of targets, the mother lode of opportunities. You could go years before you would ever find something as delicious as this," he said as he continued to stare.

"Please Tony whatever it is, don't draw any more attention to us then we already have," Tommy pleaded.

"Yeah Tony, why don't we get out of here and find someplace to eat. I'm getting hungry," Marco added trying to divert Tony's attention.

"Chuck, this is going to be a lot of fun. I invite your attention to your 9 o'clock, at an azimuth of about 270°. Behold, I spy a real war hero," Tony said without acknowledging either Tommy's or Marco's comments.

Chuck turned slowly to his left, in the direction Tony indicated." Oh my. It's perfect," he said when he saw what Tony had been staring at." He's resplendent and bemedaled."

"A very apt description my learned friend. He is resplendent and bemedaled", Tony said without removing his eyes from the man he was staring at.

"I can't determine all of his awards from this distance. However, based on the number of hash marks on his arm, he must've been in Vietnam for close to ten years," Chuck said gleefully.

In unison, they both rose and made their way through the crowd toward a booth in the far corner of the pub. Neither man spoke. Their gaze was fixed intently on their target, like two lions stalking a gazelle.

The object of their attention was a man sitting in the center of the booth flanked by two attractive young women. He wore the uniform of an army major. His arms and hands moved expressively, emphasizing a story he was relating to his companions.

As Tony and Chuck approached the booth, the man stop telling his story and looked up at the two intruders." May I help you gents," he asked.

"Why yes you can," Tony was the first to answer." We were with our friends over there," Tony pointed across the restaurant to his companions who he could see we're watching him intently."My friend Chuck and I are enormous fans of the military. In fact, we've read and studied many facets of the US military and consider ourselves quite knowledgeable about all aspects of our Armed Forces," Tony said as he and Chuck squeezed into the booth next to the two women.

A momentary look of uncertainty replaced the confident air the major had exhibited just a moment before. He looked apprehensively around the restaurant as if trying to assess possible avenues of escape. However, he was hemmed in by both the women and now Tony and Chuck.

"Given our interest in the military, we thought we could get some good first-hand information from a real hero," Chuck said innocently." Oh by the way, forgive us for the intrusion, but we both thought this was too good an opportunity to pass up," Chuck said as he extended his hand.

"I'm George," The major said as he shook Chuck's hand and reached out to shake Tony's hand also.

George relaxed slightly." I am no hero," he said looking at one of the women.

"Oh come now," Tony said earnestly."Those medals on your chest say that you're quite the hero." He pointed for emphasis at the man's chest full of awards.

George seemed to relax further after Tony's compliment. The girls, somewhat surprised by the interruption also seemed to relax. He looked down at his chest and said," Well I …….."

"Only one thing confuses me. Actually, several things confuse me," Tony interrupted him. For one thing, you're wearing a green beret. It's bad manners to wear a cover indoors."

George stiffened at Tony's criticism of him. He hesitated, then slowly removed his beret, smiling sheepishly at the two women sitting beside him.

"That's better," Tony said." Just because you Special Forces guys eat snakes doesn't mean that you have to act boorish around civilized folks like these refined ladies here.

As if on signal, both Tony and Chuck squeezed in closer to the women attempting to get closer to George."Something else doesn't seem right to me major," Chuck added. George turned his head to look at him. A panicked look momentarily crossed his face. Chuck reached around the woman at George's side and poked him in the right shoulder." This patch says you were in the First Cav in Vietnam.

Why aren't you wearing a Special Forces patch if you're wearing a Green Beret?"

The women looked from Chuck to George, confused by the change in the tone of the conversation. "Maybe we should get going Deb. Remember we told Sally we'd meet her at 6:30," one of the women said as she picked up her purse from the seat and pushed against Chuck to get out of the booth.

"Oh too bad you have to go. I believe you'd learn a lot about your friend's heroic service if you stayed. But, we all certainly understand when duty calls," Chuck slid out of the booth and allowed the woman to leave while Tony did the same thing on the other side of the booth.

"I should be going myself," George said as he slid across the booth trying to follow the women.

Before he could move very far, both Chuck and Tony returned to the booth, trapping George. "Not so fast, major. We've barely begun to explore your obviously storied military career. You wouldn't want to deprive Chuck and me of hearing of your derring-do and other courageous exploits, now would you George?" Tony moved right up against him while Chuck crowded him from the other side.

George's eyes got larger and the look of panic returned as he looked from side to side at both men. He then looked at the two women and gave a slight nod of his head toward the bar, giving them a signal to alert the management to his predicament.

Tony noticed the subtle signal. He raised his hand to get the attention of his friends across the pub, which was not difficult because they had been closely watching Chuck and Tony. Tony pointed to the two women who remained standing in front of the booth trying to decide what to do. With a series of hand signals, he directed his friends to intercept and escort the women out of the establishment. He could see Tommy and Freddie spring out of their chairs and move swiftly toward the women as they were attempting to push their way through the crowd to the bar. Tony watched as his friends met the girls, smiled and engaged them in conversation. He could see his friends point to the booth where he was sitting. Even in the distance he could see the girls relax as the four of them began to laugh. Soon both men and the two women made their way out of the bar and were lost to view.

Tony turned back to George who was also watching the movements of the two women. His frustration on seeing them fail to reach the management personnel near the bar was evident in the expression on his face.

"Looks like your friends met some nice guys on their way out of the bar," Tony said cheerfully. "Now where were we?" Tony slapped the major on the shoulder.

"We were about to hear stories of derring-do," Chuck said as he slapped George on the other shoulder.

George looked from Chuck to Tony and then at the doorway where his friends had departed.

"Oh they'll be fine. Don't you worry about them. Let's get back to your uniform and what it might tell us about your derring-do," Tony said as he poked at the ribbons on George's chest. "For instance, this silver star speaks for itself. They just don't give them to anyone. Chuck here got his because he destroyed a machine gun position after he had been wounded. Saved a bunch of his men who were pinned down. That's some real derring-do George. How did you get yours?" Tony said poking the major again in the chest.

"Well I…," George stammered.

"Look Tony he also has a Purple Heart. Did you get that when you got the Silver star?"

George turned to face Chuck." Well I…"

"Yeah but Chuck, the Purple Heart and Silver Star are out of order. The Silver Star should be here," Tony said as he poked at George's chest more forcefully.

"And there are never any V devices on Silver stars," Chuck said as he plucked off a tiny V device which had been affixed to the Silver Star ribbon." You can only get a silver star for valor, so the V is redundant. It's like saying your rank is officer major all majors are officers."

George was now in full panic mode as his eyes darted quickly from Chuck to Tony and back again. He twisted and kneaded his Green Beret between his sweaty hands.

"How long were you in Vietnam George?" Tony asked sharply.

"Um-uh- two years," George answered hesitatingly.

"Well, the nine hash marks say you were there for four and a half years. Who's lying George you or your uniform?" Tony thrust his face closer to the now fully flustered major.

"Wait Tony, let the man tell his story," Chuck said as he patted the ribbons on George's chest while gently straightening out his uniform blouse.

"Okay, let's have it George. Start from the beginning. How did you get your commission, when did you get to Vietnam, what units were you with, where were you and when were you there?" Tony's questions came quickly. He then sat back glaring at George.

George looked at Tony for a moment, then looked down at his hands which held his now rumpled and misshapen beret. He gave an audible sigh and looked first at Chuck and then at Tony. It seemed to both men that George at that instant had decided how we could extricate himself from the awkward position he found himself in. He smiled weakly while looking at Tony," Look fellas, I know you're on to me. I never was in Vietnam. I got this uniform and everything else through the mail. But, I never intended to hurt anyone by posing as a veteran. I only did it to impress the ladies and some youngsters in my neighborhood. Believe me when I tell you I never wanted to hurt anyone. The whole thing just got away from me once I started wearing the uniform. People kept asking me questions, so I had to make up answers. I didn't mean to take anything away from what you guys did. It's just that people were so nice to me and so respectful when I have this uniform on. No one ever respected me like that before. I was hooked and didn't know how to stop. You have to believe me. I didn't want to hurt anyone," George was pleading as he looked from Tony to Chuck and back again.

Tony continued to stare at George, his jaw set. He didn't say a word for a moment. When he spoke, his voice sounded like a low growl." Listen to me George, or whatever your name is, listen carefully. I'm going to try very hard not to rip off every badge and ribbon you have on that uniform and thereby expose you publicly right now to all of these unknowledgeable civilians.

By your little charade you have dishonored every brave American who honestly earned those ribbons. We're not talking about a participation award or a good attendance award, we're talking about folks who risked their lives. They did what they did not for ribbons or medals but for their buddies and an ideal bigger than themselves," Tony's voice was rising now.

"They got those ribbons and medals so the rest of the country and their comrades in the military might gain a small understanding of the sacrifices they made. For you see George, " Tony poked the major in the chest for emphasis,"Unlike you, the men who earned these medals would never tell anyone what they did. They let the ribbons tell the rest of us, in a very subtle way, how courageous they were."

Tony took a deep breath and looked down at his hands. He was silent for a moment. When he looked up Chuck could see that his face had changed from anger to sorrow. He looked off in the distance, not focusing on anything in particular. When he spoke, he spoke almost in a whisper. The earlier growl was now replaced by a reverent softness. He sighed again as he turned to George. His shoulders seemed to sag as he spoke." Here's the deal George. Many of the guys who honestly earned those ribbons that you're wearing, never got to put them on their uniforms. The only time anyone saw them was when they were shown at their funerals," Tony looked away again.

When he looked back at George, the anger on his face had returned."So here's how it's going to be Georgie boy."

The Major's eyes got bigger. Fear was evident on his face as he awaited Tony's judgment.

"Here's how it's going to be," Tony repeated for emphasis."You have two choices. You can take off all those ribbons and the major's leaves and the branch insignia. Chuck here will then cut off the First

Cav patch from your right shoulder while you sit quietly watching him defrock you. Or…" Tony's voice was rising,"I'll forcibly rip the ribbons and insignia off your uniform before Chuck and I escort you out of this restaurant and throw you on to the street. Are those two choices clear enough to you major? Do you have any questions?"

"No… Sir," George stammered as he reached inside his uniform and began to unclasp the ribbons.

Tony never took his eyes off him as George continued to remove the rank and other insignia from his uniform.

When he was finished, Chuck removed a penknife from his pocket and proceeded to cut the threads from the large Horsehead patch on George's right shoulder.

"There, that's better," Chuck said looking at the arm of the uniform, now shorn of the 1st Cavalry patch. Threads hung from the sleeve showing the vague outline of the now removed patch.

"Okay, major whatever your name is. Leave the beret here and get out of here," Tony made a motion toward the door.

Chuck slid out of the booth to allow George to leave." I'll bet you feel a lot lighter without all those ribbons and brass on your uniform," he said as he patted George lightly on his back.

"I'll bet his conscience feels a lot lighter now that he's not living a lie," Tony added. "Here's the deal, George. We'll be around watching you. If we ever catch you impersonating a hero again we'll rip off more than parts of your uniform. Is that clear?" Tony had to yell after George who was moving quickly to the door.

CHAPTER TWELVE

RUDY

"Well here it is at last," Tony announced, "The Twin Palms Racket Club, one of the most prestigious tennis addresses in the country. The founder of this club is Rudy Baer. He's developed more champions here than any other pro in the country, maybe in the world. He trains players from seven to seventy and makes champions out of all of them" That's why I think he can do something, even with you Marco."

"Thanks for the compliment, I think Tony." Marco said glumly."I'm sure he's just waiting inside to cancel all of his other lessons in order to fulfill your fantasy of seeing Barrington Howell humbled."

"It sure looks expensive Tony. You sure we have enough money for this?" Tommy asked.

"Sure, sure, don't worry," Tony answered quickly.

"'How did you get Marco scheduled so quickly Tony? I'll bet this guy is booked months ahead," Chuck chimed in.

"Well, he's really not scheduled, at least not yet. Boy, look at this layout," Tony pointed expansively as he tried to divert the group's attention.

"Wait a minute, wait a minute. What do you mean he's not scheduled just yet," Chuck moved closer to Tony.

Tony could sense the others in the van were staring at him awaiting his answer." Well, it's just that it's so hard to get through to these guys, you know because they're so famous. I thought the best thing would be to talk to him face to face. You just can't get your point across to people like this over the phone," Tony said uneasily.

Tony's obvious discomfort and vagueness seemed only to anger his companions more." Crap Tony, I can't believe you would drag us half way across the country without a better plan than this. There's no way a place like this is going to let Marco in without some advance reservation. Even your bullshit isn't going to get us out of this. If only you would have told us before this, maybe we could have figured something out. Now we're screwed," Chuck said angrily.

"Easy Chuck. We'll figure something out. Tony was just doing what he thought was right. Nothing says that this is the only place Marco can train. I'll bet Texas is loaded with places like this one. We'll go in here and get a directory or something that'll tell us where else we can go. We have been in worse situations then this and have come out okay," Tommy said trying to break the tension.

Tony's face was grim as he parked the car in the designated visitors area of the parking lot. People of all ages dressed in tennis attire, were walking through the area on their way to numerous tennis courts a short distance away. The club and the people they saw all had an air of organization and purpose.

"I don't know what it is, but this place reminds me of airborne school," Freddy said cheerfully.

"Yeah, me too," Tommy added." Only some of these troopers have better legs than I seem to remember seeing at Benning."

"That must be the headquarters," Marco said pointing to a large, one story building set amongst palm trees and well manicured landscaping.

"Well, let's go in and give it the old 1st of the 14th try," Tommy said as he put his arms around Tony and Chuck." And I want you guys to kiss and make up. We need to be shoulder to shoulder on this deal. What do you say?"

There was a short, awkward pause. Then Tony looked up and said sheepishly," Does it have to be on the lips?"

"You jerk," Chuck said good-naturedly as he hugged Tony." I'm sorry I lost my temper. That always happens to me when I drive 2000 miles with assholes."

"It's okay pal. I should have shared everything with you guys. I wanted this whole thing to come off so much that I was afraid not having it all worked out would give Marco here a better chance to chicken out," Tony said sincerely." Besides Chuck, you've given me inspiration to reach deep inside me to the innermost core of my body where the fountain of bullshit resides and bring forth my greatest effort."

"Only Tony could make bullshit sound almost Shakespearean," Freddie said with a smile.

"Our good buddy is right. Wasn't it Mark Anthony who said, 'Friends Romans and countrymen, let me tell you some bullshit,"

Tony spoke over his shoulder as he marched resolutely to the building's entrance.

The men walked up a few steps and entered into a huge reception area. The interior of the building was almost as sunny and bright as it had been outside. Plants were in abundance everywhere. An attractive, tanned young woman sat behind a huge, round desk just inside the entrance. A large waterfall fell from the ceiling into a pool behind her. The men could see spacious corridors which extended to the left and right of her beyond the waterfall.

They hesitated just inside the entrance, somewhat intimidated by what they saw." Okay, let's do it. This place ain't so hot. As a matter fact, it reminds me a little of a YMCA I visited in Newark, New Jersey once," Tony said bravely.

"And you remind me of Custer's last instructions to his troops, 'Take no prisoners'," Chuck whispered as he pushed Tony forward.

"Miss, I don't know if you noticed, but you have a leak in your roof," Tony said with a grin.

"Thank you for your astute observation. Now, is there some way I may help you?" The woman answered without a smile.

"I think Tony's innermost core must have come up dry," Tommy said quietly to his companions.

"Well actually, there is. You see, my friend over there is interested in enrolling in one of your crash programs to become a world-class tennis player," Tony said pointing at Marco.

"Is this serious now or is this a continuation of your clever opening?" the young woman said with an icy stare.

"Excuse me ma'am, but are you originally from New Jersey?" Tony asked.

"Yes I am. How could you tell?" she asked.

"Oh, just a hunch," Tony said, half turning to his companions." And in answer to your question, we are serious about enrolling our friend. It's a long story, it's very important to all of us that he get the best training possible. And from what we've heard, he can get that here."

"Well, you're right. Twin Palms is one of the finest tennis training schools in the country. I'll also take your word that it's a long story," she said coldly." Why don't you take a seat and I'll see if someone can help you."

Tony joined his friends who were already sitting in the reception area." What did she say Tony?" Tommy asked as he sat down.

"She said she was from New Jersey and you looked like a stud from Texas, only smaller," Tony said with a grin.

"Could somebody translate that for me?" Tommy asked plaintively.

"It means he didn't get to first base. I'm not enrolled and we ought to be getting an early start on our 2000 mile return trip," Marco answered somewhat sarcastically.

"Not so fast Gorgonzola breath," Tony said confidently. "She's sending someone out to see us. So, why don't we just sit here and enjoy the scenery until 'Mr. Big' gets here."

"Yeah, it's kind of nice in here after riding in that cramped van all night. And, watching all these pretty girls isn't too bad. Besides that waterfall kind of relaxes me," Chuck said with a sigh.

"It makes me want to go to the bathroom,"Freddie said."It reminds me of how my mother would run the water in the sink when I was young to get me to go to the bathroom before I went to bed."

"I'm sure the architects of this building would be pleased to know that they spent several million dollars on this place and its major impact was on your bladder," Tony said with a smirk."Who says we ain't got no couth in our group? "

"Hey Tony, I think that guy rumbling toward us could be your man," Freddie nodded his head.

Tony looked up to see a tall, muscular, tanned man striding toward them. He moved fluidly and gracefully, a slight frown on his face.

"Hi, I'm Biff. Beverly told me you gentlemen had some questions," the man greeted them.

"Yes we do have some questions. The first one is that I thought there was a federal law against anyone over 25 having the name Biff or Chip," Tony said with a smile.

"Nah, I think it was repealed in Texas. And I think Muffie is still legal in Boston and upstate New York," Chuck added.

"Ah, Beverly mentioned you were playful. I can see now what she meant," Biff answered with a sarcastic grin." But seriously, what can I do for you gentlemen?"

"Well, it's very important that our friend here gets enrolled in your school. Marco, come and meet Biff," Tony motioned to his friend." It's very important to all of us that Marco become the best tennis player he can become in the next two weeks. We've driven

2000 miles to you guys here because we heard you were the best in the country."

"Well, I know I speak for Mr. Baer and the whole staff when I say that we're flattered to learn of your efforts. Unfortunately, the school is completely booked up now. The earliest to get your friend in is probably three months from now. Why don't you get an application from Bev and we can contact you when there's an opening," Biff said as he turned to go.

Tony grabbed his arm."Listen, this is important. Marco's not trying to win some puny club championship. This match is very important to a lot of people. There must be some way you can fit him in."

Biff pulled his arm away and scowled at Tony, "Well, I'll certainly try, he said flatly. "Why don't you leave me the local number where you'll be staying and I'll call you if anything comes up. Perhaps we can fit your friend into one of our group lessons."

"Yeah, okay, Biff why don't we try that. I'll go out to the van and get the telephone number and give it to Beverly, if that's all right," Tony said with a tight smile.

Tony returned to his friends as Biff walked over to the receptionist." What happened Tony?" Tommy asked as he got closer.

"We got the bum's rush from Prince Charming over there. Without staring, let me know when he leaves," Tony said grimly."Now I am really pissed. Marco's going to get a good hearing before we leave this place."

"Tony, let's just find another place. There's no sense in making a scene here," Marco pleaded.

"Okay Tony, he's going, but he must have told the iceberg up there to watch us because she's really giving you the eye," Chuck reported as he watched Biff leave the reception area.

"Okay Tom, I want you to create a diversion near her so I can find the big guy and plead our case," Tony said without looking around.

"You've got it pal. When I get done diverting, you'll be able to drive the van in here without her noticing," Tommy responded. He then walked slowly toward the receptionist staring at her and smiling broadly. She watched him warily while glancing at his friends periodically. He circled the desk, still looking directly at the now puzzled receptionist. As he backed away, Tommy knocked over one of the large potted plants adorning the reception area. In trying to right the it , Tommy tripped and fell to the floor, spilling a good portion of the dirt in the pot. Several people including the receptionist, tried to help Tommy who was by now slipping on the spilled dirt and pulling others to the floor.

"Tommy was right," Tony said with a grin."Go get the van and drive it in here Marco."

"If you're going to do your thing, you'd better do it before the one-man Marx Brothers finishes his act," Chuck urged.

"You're right Chuck. I'm out of here," Tony said as he made his way down one of the corridors. He moved quickly, half expecting to be challenged by someone who might have seen him leave the reception area. After a few moments, he slowed down and nodded to the people he encountered in the hallway so he wouldn't draw attention. He soon determined that the corridor he was in formed the perimeter of the building. He took notice of the numerous offices located on both sides of the hallway.

He knew that corporate culture dictated that the chief executive had the corner office. He hoped that tennis culture had a similar idiosyncrasy. He soon came to an open area which looked like a mini version of the reception area he had left moments before. Tony stopped at a water fountain and took a long drink. This allowed him to catch his breath and survey the surrounding area. Looking beyond the receptionist in this area he saw a large office with the plaque which read 'Rudy Baer, Director'. His heart beat faster as he tried to formulate his plan.

For the first time in as long as Tony could remember, he was at a loss as to what to do next. He could feel himself panicking as he tried to focus on how he could tell his story to Rudy Baer. The long trip and the initial rebuff in the reception area were taking their toll on him. However, the full realization that he had dragged his friends across the country in order to carry out a poorly thought out and maybe impossible task, shook his confidence. Tony couldn't remember the last time he had felt this uncertain, but he knew he didn't like it.

He momentarily considered retracing his steps to where his friends were still waiting. He could tell them that Rudy Baer wasn't in and maybe they should find another club that would be more receptive to their plan. As he considered his next action, the door to Rudy Baer's office opened. A short, stocky, almost pudgy man came out smiling and joking, accompanied by an attractive well-dressed, middle-aged woman. They kissed goodbye. The woman walked quickly past Tony while the man paused to talk to another woman, obviously his secretary. He then turned and walked back into his office.

Without thinking or waiting, Tony walked past the secretary and followed the man into his office. He could vaguely hear the woman challenging and protesting as he brushed by her. Tony didn't look around but sensed that she had followed him into the office. He couldn't be sure since he was focusing so intently on the man. Rudy Baer turned and faced him, a broad smile on his face. He seemed quite amused by the unexpected commotion in his office.

"I'm sorry Mr. Baer, this gentleman just barged in. I wasn't able to stop him," the secretary said breathlessly.

"Oh that's okay Jennie, I'll see what he wants," Rudy Baer said good-naturedly. He seemed almost to welcome the distraction.

"Well, okay Mr. Baer. I'll be right outside if you need me," Jennie said uncertainly.

"Why don't you sit down, Mr. Um-uh. I'm sorry, I didn't get your name," Rudy invited.

"Tony, Tony DeJulio, Mr. Baer. I'm sorry to have barged in on you like this," Tony stammered.

"Oh that's okay Tony. Actually I wasn't ready to get back to work just yet. My wife just left and she always tells me I'm too intense and work too hard. She'd be happy to know I didn't just dive back into work," Rudy said with a smile.

Because of Rudy's easy-going and cordial manner, Tony was beginning to relax and regain his composure." Well, I'll tell you Mr. Baer, for as nice a guy as you are, you sure are surrounded by a bunch of folks who aren't nearly as friendly."

"Call me Rudy, okay? Yeah, I know I have some people who think more highly of themselves and their positions then they have a right to. But, for the most part we have nice people. You just ran into a few of the Dobermans around here who think I need to be protected," Rudy chuckled. "But tell me, how can I help you."

"Well, Mr. Baer, um I mean Rudy, I know you're a busy guy so I'll get right to the point. I came here with several other guys. We all were in Vietnam together. One of them, Marco, has been challenged by some pablum puking wimp, draft dodging jerk, to a tennis match. Now, if it were just a tennis match, we wouldn't have driven across the country to try to get you to help us. But, this whole thing has become a public issue where we work, maybe in the whole town. People have started to take sides. I don't want to sound overly dramatic, but this is shaping up as a contest between good and evil, haves and have-nots in avoiding responsibility and service to the country. And, if that's not enough, there's a girl involved," Tony said seriously.

"Hardly sounds overly dramatic to me," Rudy chuckled again. "We are probably only talking about the beginning of the decline of Western civilization as we know it."

"Yeah, I think that could happen too if Marco loses this match," Tony said with a grin.

"So, you think I can help your friend Marco whip the pablum puker. Well, Tony I'm pretty good, but a lot will depend on how bad your friend is and how good the other guy is. I certainly don't want to cause the decline of civilization, but I can't always work miracles. If I decided to help you how much time would I have to work this miracle?"

"You could have as much time as you need Rudy, as long as it doesn't take over two weeks. The match is in three weeks and we need time to get home," Tony was ecstatic that Rudy seemed interested in helping him.

"Okay Tony, I'll tell you what I'll do. I'll take a look at your friend's ability tomorrow. If I think there's any hope, I'll take on the job. I'm not promising anything. I really can't afford to have my name or my school associated with a fiasco. When word gets out, and it will, that I had a hand in this thing, it has to look professional. As long as you understand that I'm going to take a close look at your friend and give him a fair chance. However, if there's no chance, I'm going to deny we ever met. Is that fair?"

"Sure is Rudy. That's very fair. More than fair. Fairer than I ever thought possible when I barged in on you," Tony said gratefully.

"Okay, let's go meet the challenge or opportunity as the case may be," Rudy said ushering Tony toward the door." Wait a minute Tony, I want to show you something," Rudy said. He walked around behind his desk and selected a framed picture from among several that were neatly arranged on his credenza.

"This is my son, also named Rudy," he said as he showed the photo to Tony." He flew F-105s in Vietnam. In July 1967, he was shot down over north Vietnam. His wing man saw Rudy eject and saw his parachute open, but that was the last time any American saw him."

Tony took the picture that Rudy handed him. It was obvious that the young man in the Air Force uniform was Rudy's son. The same broad smile and impish twinkle in his eyes was readily recognizable." I'm sorry Rudy," Tony said as he handed the picture back." I can say because of the friends I lost, that I understand your grief to some degree. I know I don't understand it fully because I know that losing a child must be devastating."

Rudy took the picture back, almost reverently and stared at it silently for a moment." I almost didn't tell you about Rudy because I made a promise to myself a long time ago to keep my emotions and sorrow private. I know that's what Rudy would've wanted. But, I also know he would have been very amused by you and your friend and this tennis match. That's really why I'm such a willing party to your scheme. I know you thought it was your eloquence that did it," Rudy said with a grin as he returned the picture carefully to the credenza.

Rudy took one last look at the photo and walked to Tony and put his arm around the younger man." Let's go whip your friend into shape," he said with a grin. His seriousness of only a moment before was gone, replaced once again by his initial enthusiasm and joviality.

As the two men left the office, they passed by Rudy's astonished secretary." My friend, Tony, and I will be out in the lobby for a short time," Rudy announced.

"Hold my messages, will you Jennie," Tony said as he walked quickly to catch up with Rudy.

"You're awful," Rudy chuckled as the two men walked down the hall.

As they approached the reception area, they could see Tony's friends being confronted by Biff and several security guards." What's going on here Biff?" Rudy asked as he walked up to the group.

Biff turned around, obviously surprised at seeing his boss." Just a little misunderstanding Mr. Baer. I'll have these guys out of here and this thing cleared up in no time," he said apologetically.

"Out of here?" Rudy said his voice rising slightly." Why these people are my special guests. I've been waiting for them to arrive since yesterday."

Biff stiffened as he stared at Rudy, trying to comprehend this sudden and unexpected turn of events." I… I'm sorry, Mr. Baer. I just didn't know," he finally blurted out.

Tony stepped from behind Rudy and said in a whisper loud enough for everyone to hear, "I tried to tell you Biff, but you wouldn't listen. I believe he's exercised too much above the neck."

"That'll be all Biff, I'll take care of my guests now," Rudy said, obviously dismissing him.

"I'm sorry again Mr. Baer," Biff said as he hurriedly left the area.

"I'll never doubt you again," Tommy said with a grin."I've seen you pull off quite a few amazing things in our time together, but this is the all-time topper. And, the timing was spectacular. Just when the Indians we're about to overrun the wagon train, the mini guinea turns up with the cavalry."

"Okay, where's the patient Tony?" Rudy asked surveying the group.

"It's the skinny, weak looking little one right here," Tony said pointing at Marco.

Marco reached out with an embarrassed grin and said,"Happy to meet you Mr. Baer. I don't know what Tony told you to get you to do this, but for whatever reason you might accept I'm grateful."

"He doesn't look quite as spastic as you told me he was," Rudy said with a loud guffaw as he took Marco's hand."I think we have a chance, only a slight one, but nonetheless a chance. I want Marco delivered to court number one at 7 AM tomorrow. I don't want the rest of you guys anywhere near court one until I tell you. Is that clear?"

"Yes sir," the group answered in unison.

"We have a great pool here on the grounds and the scenery is pretty nice," Rudy said with a wink." I can have Jennie leave passes for all of you at the front desk if you like."

"Rudy that would be great. And, we'll have Marco here at seven o'clock sharp," Tony answered. Turning to Marco he said," You lucky stiff. You'll be training with one of the country's best tennis pros at one of the world's best tennis facilities while we sit around a hot swimming pool surrounded by beautiful women we don't even know. It's a dirty, rotten job, but somebody has to do it." They all laughed as they crowded around Marco, slapping him on the back.

CHAPTER THIRTEEN

TRAINING

As they approached the court, Tony and his friends could see Marco scurrying from side to side trying to return balls hit by a ball machine." Wow, it's got to be 95 degrees out. Rudy has Marco working out harder than we did in Airborne school. Look at his shirt. It's soaked," Chuck said sympathetically."Maybe we should hide these drinks and ask the girls to go back to the pool."

"Absolutely not," Tony said emphatically." Marco always does better when he gets to be the martyr. It's an Italian genetic trait. This will really piss him off, then he'll practice harder. Watch."

Rudy interrupted Marco's hitting to give him some instructions. From his animated gestures, it was clear that Rudy was trying to get Marco to move quickly to where the ball was before attempting to hit it. Both Rudy and Marco noticed the group approaching the court at the same time. With a pat on the back, Rudy sent Marco back to his position at the baseline to resume hitting balls. As he walked slowly toward the fence surrounding the court he continued to watch Marco closely while moving toward Tony and his assembled friends.

"What do you think Rudy? How's he doing?" Tony asked as the coach approached the fence.

"I believe he's got some real talent that I can develop," Rudy answered." I haven't told him that though. I told him that he was one of the hardest cases I've ever had. He's out of shape, but he's a hard worker so I think I can have him whipped into shape in the vast two weeks you've allotted me," Rudy smiled.

"That's good news. He played in high school, but he hasn't played in such a long time I was worried about his ability to revive his skills. I knew you could work miracles, but even you need some raw material to start with", Tony sighed with relief.

"Boy, he's really moving and smacking the ball now. You're right Tony." Tommy observed.

"Yeah, he did seem to get more motivated when he saw all of you," Rudy mused." Maybe you should come every morning and afternoon to inspire him. I think we can use as many forms of motivation as we can get. For instance, you mentioned a girl yesterday."

"Yeah, Kathy. Marco's a pretty private guy, but I know him well enough to know that he's smitten. The opponent in this match, El Waspo, is also interested in Kathy. And since he's a smooth, rich guy, she kind of likes him. That's another reason why this match is so important," Tony added.

"Okay, that's good information. Now you guys buzz off, but be back here this afternoon at 4:00 o'clock for the same kind of motivation session. Marco really seems to work harder when you're here."

"You've got it. Anything we can do to help, even if it means spending time with these tennis rejects that hang around the pool. I know you're only interested in serves and backhands and therefore probably haven't noticed that these young ladies have some other redeeming features," Tony said with a grin.

"You're right. I only care about size of hands for tennis grips. And, for two weeks, that's all I want Marco to care about. So, no matter what you guys do, I want Marco in his room when he's not with me. I want you and him to always remember that he's in training. Anything less in the short time we have, won't work." Rudy said solemnly.

"Count on me Rudy. I'll make sure that Marco's two weeks here will make a monk's existence seem like 'Lifestyles of the Rich and Famous,'" Tony said with a smile.

CHAPTER FOURTEEN

JUSTINE

Justine saw him first. He was standing in the entrance to the small, crowded bar looking for her. It took a moment for her eyes to become accustomed to the dim light of the interior of the room. She studied him briefly, grateful for the extra time she had before he noticed her. His hair was slightly gray and he somehow looked older, but he was unmistakably Tony. She signaled him with a wave of her hand about the same time he saw her. She got up as he made his way across the crowded room. She hesitated a moment and then extended her hand in greeting.

Tony took her hand and swept her up in a hug, kissing her on the cheek. *That was unmistakably Tony too. He had the unique ability to almost immediately establish physical contact with everyone, men and women. He did it with such ease that no one ever seemed to be offended by it. Tony's ability to disarm almost everyone in this way was one of his major strengths, she thought. She envied his ability to do it and attributed it to his Italian background. She was never comfortable hugging people because of her own upbringing which frowned upon any physical contact between all but the closest of family members.*

"Boy, do you look great," Tony said enthusiastically. Any doubts Justine had about the meeting evaporated in the face of Tony's hug, smile and genuine pleasure at seeing her again.

"I'll bet you say that to all of your old Army buddies," Justine replied with a broad smile.

"Yeah, I do," Tony replied." But with you, I mean it. Some of the other guys could win a Pillsbury Doughboy look-alike contest now. They're far from the lean warriors they once were."

"Oh really! Who have you seen? I'm dying to know who you're in contact with," Justine said excitedly.

"Well, actually I'm out here with a bunch of the old guys. Marco, Freddy, Chuck, Bob and Tom. Do you remember those guys?"

"Well, you know Marco was always one of my favorites. You introduced me to those other guys a few times, but I don't remember them as well. How is Marco?" Justine asked as they sat down.

"He hasn't changed a bit Justine. I would have brought him, but he's in training over at a tennis club in Dallas"

"Wait a minute. Training at a tennis club? I think this update is going to take even longer than I had anticipated. Maybe I should call my office and tell them I won't be back for the rest of the afternoon," Justine said with a smile.

"The rest of the afternoon? Are you kidding? The rest of the afternoon will only get us to 1972. I don't know about you, but I've had a pretty exciting life since we last saw each other," Tony replied with a smirk.

"'Well let's try. I only have one week of vacation left, so I might only be able to get to 1979 this trip. Start with why you're in Dallas and Marco's tennis training."

"You remember that Marco is the nicest guy in the whole world and normally lets people walk all over him. Some big-time executive in our company insulted him once too often about being a baby killer in Vietnam. Marco came an inch away from using his Ranger training to demonstrate to a bunch of insurance workers the more gruesome side of his experience. Instead of ripping his heart out, we decided on a more genteel, civil competition-tennis," Tony explained."Oh, by the way, there's also a girl at stake in all of this."

"Okay, now I've got it. 'We' decided on a tennis match means that you arranged the match. And, with your normal flair for the understatement, you dragged Marco here to be trained at one of those world-class tennis finishing schools. Of course, if 'we' challenged him 'we' aren't going to lose are 'we'?" Justine rested her chin on her folded hands and studied Tony's face.

"You always could always figure me out better than anyone else in the world," Tony said sheepishly. "But enough about me and this trip. I'm dying to hear what you've been up to. I see by your left-hand that you're engaged. I couldn't find a Justine O'Reilly in the Dallas phone book. If I hadn't remembered that your parents lived here, I would never have found you. Your mom seemed genuinely pleased that an old Army friend would be looking for you."

"She's mellowed considerably since my army days. I told you in Vietnam how she was opposed to my going into the army. Now she seems almost proud of my service, especially my Vietnam tour. It's amazing how time and distance can change everyone's perspective," Justine said with a wry smile.

"And what about your fiancé? How does he feel being engaged to a combat hardened veteran?"

"Well, you know Tony, it's a nonevent. We never talk about it. He was in law school during the war so he never thought much about it when it was going on. He didn't demonstrate against the war or anything like that. Since he knew he wouldn't have to go, he kind of ignored it. I think that irritates me more than anything. I sometimes wish he had been passionate about it one way or another. Although I'm sure I wouldn't have been attracted to him if he had told me he was an antiwar demonstrator. Actually, I'm not sure I could've lived with someone who was in Vietnam either. I think it's kind of comfortable this way with Ned. I'm not reminded of the war in any way. That way, I get to control when I think about Vietnam."

"And what do you do for a living? Are you still in the hospital business?" Tony seemed to be studying Justine more intensely, looking for any facial expression or body language that could help him understand more fully e very word she spoke.

"Nope, I took all of the valuable hospital experience and training I got in the Army and became a stockbroker," Justine said with a laugh.

"A stockbroker? Come on Justine, you were one of the best in your business. The Army had you on a fast track for early promotion. And I know you loved the hospital business. You always talked about going home and continuing your career in the states. What happened?"

"Well, you're one of the few guys who realized I wasn't a nurse. In Vietnam, we were always so shorthanded, we all did what had to be done. But, I was really a Medical Services Officer. When I came home, I got several offers to get into hospital administration. I even toyed with the idea of becoming a nurse. But, after that year in Vietnam, I had no real desire to be around hospitals again. You know it's funny. I volunteered to go to Vietnam because I felt I needed some intensity in my life, something to really care about. Well, I found so much intensity and I cared so much over there, I think there was nothing left when I came home. Nothing has ever been as important to me and I don't think it ever will be again," Justine said sadly looking down at her clasped hands.

"I know exactly what you mean," Tony said reaching over to touch Justine's hand.

"I've never felt as needed as I was over there. But, that's probably why I'm protecting myself from those kinds of responsibilities. I think the burden of caring for all of those young soldiers away from home, was too much for me. I wasn't much older than they were and yet, I had to be understanding and cheerful even when I didn't understand and wasn't happy." She stared across the room for a moment." But, that's why I'm a stockbroker now," She said cheerily, breaking the mood." If IBM goes down a few points, it's not the end of the world. Although some of my clients think it is," she said with a grin.

Tony didn't say anything for a moment, "You know, I believe the reason we got so close so quickly in Vietnam was because we were so much alike. After all these years, it's funny that your description of how you feel is exactly how I feel. It's very hard for me to get very intense or serious about anything. Earlier this year, my favorite uncle died. I loved that guy. From the time I was a little kid until he died, he and I had a special bond. But you know when he died, I didn't feel sad. I tried real hard to feel said, but I just couldn't. Sure, I miss him, but I didn't feel sad. I kept thinking at his funeral, that he lived to be 83. That's 65 more years than some of the young guys in my unit ever got."

Justine and Tony sat silently for a moment, holding hands. Tony spoke first." What happened to us Justine? We were so close so much in love over there and yet it ended so quickly once we got home."

"You know I used to think about that a lot," Justine looked up and stared into Tony's eyes." I finally figured out that I think neither of us wanted to know if we really were in love or if it was the war and our situation that made us think we were in love. I didn't want to destroy the one beautiful piece of that very sad year for me. It's almost as if I packaged and wrapped up a valuable memento and put it away. I would have been heartbroken if it had gotten tarnished or I found out it was a fake. I never wanted to find out. I want always to believe that it was a priceless gift. I thought that If I never show it to anyone, even the giver, I'd never have to know the real answer. The beautiful perception and precious image will stay intact. And that's very important to me Tony." For the first time since they'd been together, Justine seemed to lose some of the cool control she had exhibited. Tears welled up in her eyes and her voice quivered as Tony squeezed her hand.

"Sometimes, especially during lonely, cold, rainy days, I allow myself to think about us in Vietnam. I just kind of bask in the warm feeling it gives me. If it starts to get away from me, I just put the memories away again and go off and do something to get my mind off it. At first, it was hard for me to do that. But, I've gotten quite good at maintaining control. Does any of this makes sense to you?" Justine asked while dabbing the tears from her eyes.

"I understand exactly," Tony said softly. "What you and I had is a distant wonderful memory. I use that memory in the same way. It kind of reminds me of when I was a little boy. I sometimes would keep a stock of candy hidden in my room. Eating the candy wasn't that important to me. Being able to secretly think about that candy was what was important. You know, it's actually hard for me to really believe that I was there for a year. Sure, I know I was there and I can remember a lot, but it almost seems that it happened to someone else. As a matter of fact, I'm almost embarrassed to tell you that I keep a picture of myself in Vietnam in my wallet. It's as if I have to prove to myself that I was there."

Justine laughed" That's really great, so do I." Justine reached into her purse at the same time that Tony pulled out his wallet. Both exchanged pictures and were silent for a moment as they looked at the old photos." What babies we were," Justine said nostalgically." Babies participating in the worst of all adult activities. Thank God, I had you for that short time. I don't know what I would've done without you to provide a beautiful light amidst all of that darkness."

Tony placed the photographs carefully on the table, reaching over to grasp Justine's hand again." You know, one of the first things that attracted me to you was the contrast between how young you were and yet how wise you were. You seemed to have a greater under-standing and maturity about what was going on. Everyone seemed to handle the stress differently. Some people went off the deep end, others did things they never would have done in the world and still others just became very introspective and silent. But, you always seemed to have an air of serenity as if you understood something about the war that the rest of us didn't. I believe it was that serenity that caused so many people to lay their problems on you. You seemed to have an infinite capacity to absorb everyone else's hardships. And even though I know you paid a heavy price for it, you helped a bunch of folks including me more than you'll ever know."

"Thanks Tony. For one brief moment, we had Camelot. And that moment will sustain me for a lifetime. I'll never forget you," Justine answered softly as she picked up the photo and returned it to her wallet.

They looked at each other in silence for a moment. Finally, Justine looked at her watch. "Oh my gosh, I've stayed far longer than I intended. By now my clients will be in an uproar. I have to get back."

"Yeah, so do I," Tony said." I have to check on Marco's progress."

Justine got up to leave with Tony still holding her hand." Just give me one of those famous O'Reilly smiles before you go. It was the first thing I saw when I came out of the anesthetic in Vietnam and I'd like it to be the last thing I see before you leave."

"Well, I don't feel much like smiling now. But, then again, I didn't really feel much like smiling that first time I saw you with all those tubes coming out of almost every opening of your body," Justine responded" How's this?" She said, attempting a smile even though she had tears in her eyes.

"It's great," Tony answered. They looked at one another for a moment. Then Justine turned abruptly and walked quickly out of the bar.

* * * *

Justine felt strangely unsettled by her meeting with Tony. After she received Tony's unexpected phone call, she tried to anticipate which emotions might be triggered by seeing him again after so many years. What she was sure of, however, was that she had compartmentalized and firmly sealed her memories of Vietnam and Tony in a lock box that only she could unlock when she chose to. Now she felt that the box had been ripped open and the memories she had so tightly controlled had spilled out.

She knew she couldn't go back to the office and deal with her clients who would be seeking her opinion and advice on that day's market activity. So instead, she drove aimlessly around before stopping at a mall where she window shopped without really seeing the merchandise.

The only firm conclusion she came to was that she felt she had to tell Ned about the meeting. She wasn't sure why she felt so strongly about that. Part of it she suspected, was because her meeting with Tony had rekindled some emotions she thought had been long buried. Because she and Ned had always had an open and honest relationship, she felt obligated to tell him something. Since she didn't understand her own emotions at that point, she decided to wait until she got home to decide how much to reveal about the impact the meeting had had on her.

She took a deep breath before she unlocked the door to her condo." Hon," she yelled as she entered the foyer.

"Back here in the kitchen," Ned answered.

"What are you making?" she asked as she kissed him on the cheek.

"Shrimp scampi," he answered without looking up from his chopping." How was your day."

"Good, really good," she said as she took off her coat and threw it over a chair." Smells good already," she added while trying to collect her thoughts. Although she had spent several hours trying to analyze her meeting with Tony and her reaction to it, she still felt unprepared about how to tell Ned about what had happened.

She picked up the mail that Ned had dropped on the little desk in the kitchen that she sometimes used instead of the office she maintained in the back bedroom. She avoided looking at Ned by sorting through the envelopes without really seeing who they were from.

"Wasn't today the day you were going to meet up with one of your old Army buddies?" Ned asked while continuing to prepare the meal.

"Um– Yeah. It was one of the guys I knew from the hospital I served at in Vietnam."

Without looking up from his dinner preparations he asked," Was it the guy in the picture you kept in your underwear drawer?"

Justine's head jerked up involuntarily. She stared at Ned who seemed very focused on sautéing garlic in a pan. She collected her thoughts for a moment before she resumed sorting through the mail.

Then she asked as casually as she could," What were you doing in my underwear drawer?"

"Several months ago, you had a COD delivery from SAKS. I didn't have any cash and I knew that's where you kept your money, so I used that to pay for the package. I just forgot to tell you. I hope that's okay. In any event, in searching for the money, I found the photo." He was staring at her now.

Justine's mind was racing. She felt warm and knew her face was flushed. She put the mail down and moved toward Ned." Sure that's okay. Do you want me to start the pasta?" She asked as casually as she could.

"No, I got it covered. Why don't you go into the living room and read the newspaper. I'll call you when everything is ready."

Justine started to leave the kitchen, anxious to recover her composure.

"Was that the guy?" Ned yelled after her. She turned to face him again."Yes, that was the guy. He had been badly wounded when I met him. He says I saved his life."

"You weren't a nurse. How did you save his life?" Ned had stopped his food preparation and was now totally focused on Justine.

She could feel anger now supplanting the unexpected surprise she had felt earlier when Ned had first confronted her." This is amazing. For two years you never expressed any interest in my time in Vietnam. Now all of a sudden tonight you've developed a keen interest in my duties over there," she said angrily.

"No Justine," Ken said calmly,"I'm not interested in your duties in Vietnam. You and I have a long-standing unspoken agreement that I wouldn't probe your Vietnam days for fear of upsetting you by rekindling some bad memories. Maybe your angry response just now was evidence that it was a good policy."

Justine look at Ned for a moment, forcing her anger to subside. His lawyerly unemotional response to all their discussions always trumped her quick Irish temper. His lack of emotion in the court room made him a very successful lawyer. At home, she found it increasingly annoying that he rarely displayed any passion for any issues they discussed.

She moved back to the desk and sat down. As calmly as she could she said,"No, I wasn't a nurse. However, we were so short-handed at times especially after big battles, that we all chipped in and did what had to be done. Tony, that's the guy I met today, needed around-the-clock care. I helped the overworked nurses give him that care. When you're drowning, whoever is perceived as getting you safely to shore, whether they deserve the full credit or not is who they remember. Metaphorically we were both drowning at the time." Justine immediately regretted saying that last sentence. She was hopeful that Ned wouldn't probe what she meant by it.

He resumed his cooking chores without looking at her."Having a close relationship under those extreme conditions is certainly understandable," he said evenly.

The smell of the garlic reached her as it sizzled and popped in the pan." You know what's funny Justine?" Without waiting for her answer he continued." What's ironic is that when I hear you discuss Vietnam with other people, your descriptions of that time have an almost whimsical quality to them. Your discussions seem to have more nostalgia than bitter memories. I can't understand that and I know I can never be part of it so I believe our first inclination to steer clear of Vietnam was the right one," he said as he dumped the linguine into the pot of boiling water.

She looked at him for a moment as if seeing him for the first time. She couldn't help but compare this discussion with the emotion packed meeting she had had with Tony a few hours earlier. She knew at that exact moment that she and Ned were finished. She didn't know yet how Tony might fit into her life, but after tonight she knew unequivocably that she had half the answer.

* * * *

For the next two weeks, the routine continued. Marco was dropped off early in the morning to meet with Rudy. They practiced various aspects of the game in the blazing morning sun until eleven o'clock. Following lunch, Marco reviewed tapes of his morning practice with Rudy or one of the other instructors who worked with him. At two in the afternoon they were back on the court to polish the parts of the game which had been uncovered during the tape review sessions. At five o'clock, Tony and his friends were on hand to take Marco back to the motel. After a meal, prescribed by the club's nutritionist, Marco went back to his room to do some limbering up exercises and watch TV.

Tony and the others were polite enough to wait until Marco fell into an exhausted sleep around eight o'clock before they went out on the town.

CHAPTER FIFTEEN

SERGEANT COLE

Tony was up well before dawn. Chuck and he left the rest of their sleeping companions silently and made their way to the parking lot of the motel. It was still dark when they arrived at the rental car agency. After a quick check to make sure that Tony's reserved car was on hand, Chuck said goodbye and was on his way back to the motel.

As he made his way past the vehicles in the agency lot, Tony was glad that he had elected to get a rental car for his trip across the West Texas prairie. Their van was by now clearly showing the strain of being the mobile repository of all of the gear and activity of his friends who had been traveling together for almost a week.

He carefully laid out the maps and the written instructions he had received from Sergeant Cole on the front seat. Traffic was sparse as he eased out of the parking lot and made his way onto the street leading to the ramp of the interstate. As an easterner, Tony was impressed that the interstate ran right through the center of Dallas and was so readily accessible from much of the city. That 'let's get going' attitude of the Texans Tony knew from the army seemed to be so clearly reflected in the city's arterial layout.

He recalled that some of the best soldiers he had served with came generally from the south and from Texas specifically. Fortunately for the Armed Forces, the respect for the military and the desire to serve continued to remain strong in the south.

He settled in behind the wheel and set the cruise control for the long, boring ride across the West Texas landscape. His mind seemed to set itself also to an automatic pilot that enabled him to recall the many fine men he had served with during his army years. It seemed to Tony that the best people America produced gravitated toward service to the country in some form. He was grateful that he had been a part of that unique brotherhood.

First Sergeant Cole was a great example of the type of soldier Tony recalled with pride, and yes a degree of fondness. He had been Marco's Field First Sergeant in Vietnam, but Tony knew him also because he was one of the strongest NCOs in the battalion.

The built up areas of Dallas began to recede and was quickly replaced by the sprawl of Arlington and then Fort Worth. The traffic increased steadily as the first rays of the morning sun appeared behind Tony. As he reached the western boundary of Fort Worth, the number of vehicles diminished considerably. The wide-open spaces of the Texas Tony had imagined became suddenly visible. He could see low hills in the distance on either side of the interstate. Scrub oak, juniper trees and yucca plants dotted the landscape closer to the road. The desert prairie spread before him both north and south of the interstate as far as the eye could see.

Tony was surprised that this hardscrabble land could have spawned such a vibrant and active economy and lifestyle almost since the arrival of the first American settlers in the 18th century.

Of course, Tony knew it was hearty people who had tamed this hostile land. And, it was the descendants of those hardy people whom Tony had met in the army and whom he admired for their toughness. And, it was Sergeant Cole who specifically embodied the best characteristics of that hardy stock.

Tony looked forward to seeing the old soldier again. Not only because he held the answers to what had happened to Marco, but because he also was another link in the brotherhood that Tony valued and missed so much.

His daydreaming almost caused Tony to miss the exit off the interstate. As he headed south on Texas Highway 206, the terrain became slightly hillier. Entrances to ranches appeared periodically on both sides of the highway. It was hard for Tony to imagine how ranchers could make a living on this hard land. "*If anyone could make it work, these tough Texans were the ones to do it,*" Tony thought.

He slowed as he reached the town limits of Cullman. A restaurant and a feed store pretty much defined the downtown area. Texas Highway 206 intersected with county road 82 West at a stop sign. Sergeant Cole's instructions directed Tony to turn right onto the County Road and proceed to a mailbox and driveway exactly 2.3 miles from the intersection. Tony was past the mailbox before he realized he had missed it. He doubled back and slowly approached the mailbox to verify that it was in fact the same address he had been given.

He turned down a gravel driveway and proceeded along a fence line. He soon saw a charming ranch house with a big barn off to the right. A pickup truck and trailer were parked near the barn so Tony followed the road in that direction. As he approached the barn, he saw several people observing some activity in a fenced in area nearby. At the sound of Tony's tires crunching on the gravel, they all turned to watch him as he parked his vehicle.

A short, muscular man with a military style haircut left the others and marched resolutely toward Tony. He recognized Sergeant Cole's swagger immediately. Almost thirty years seemed to have had no effect on the firmness or quickness of the sergeant's movements. Tony barely got out of his vehicle before Sergeant Cole was upon him.

"How are you doing sir?" He said as he gripped Tony's hand and slapped him on the arm at the same time. "It's awfully nice of you to drive all that distance to visit me. I don't get many visitors out here, so I'm always glad to get one, especially one from those glory days of long ago," he said smiling broadly.

Tony stepped back and looked at his friend. He was as lean and trim as he had been in Vietnam. His sun-tanned face revealed a few more wrinkles then Tony remembered, but the confident gaze and friendly smile were the same.

"You look like you could still do twenty repetitions of the daily dozen if you had to," Tony said looking again at the trim body and muscular arms of his friend.

"Well, thank you. Keeping up with a 200 acre ranch will do that for you. If you want to sign on as a ranch hand here, I can get you back to your Vietnam fighting trim in a few weeks," Sergeant Cole laughed.

"Nope, I'm beyond saving. Creature comfort has me firmly in its grasp, and I'm enjoying it," Tony smiled.

Both men stood silently and looked at the other for a moment. Almost simultaneously they stepped forward and embraced in a big bear hug."It's so good to see you again old friend," Tony said as he stepped back to look at Sergeant Cole again.

"Yup, there's nothing like seeing a comrade from those long-ago days. Actually, the last time I saw you, you weren't looking so good. You might not even remember it, but I came to visit you at the MASH after you got wounded in that dumb operation we had in November. I was with my C.O. Captain Covello."

"I vaguely remember your visit. I was so doped up for about a week, I hardly remember anything from those early hospital days. Lieutenant O'Reilly, the Medical Services Officer I knew in the MASH, filled me in when I finally regained my senses."

"Oh! I thought she was a nurse. She sure did hover around you the whole time we were there. It looked like you were getting some very special attention from a very attractive woman. Too bad you were out of it. You were the envy of everyone else in that ward," Sergeant Cole gave out a long guffaw.

"Yup. I know I was a lucky man. Lieutenant O'Reilly stayed with me for my whole recovery which lasted over two months. But, that was then and this is now. I came all this way to hear more about you and your C.O. Captain Covello and what happened to A company during that dumb operation as you call it."

"I know you and Captain Covello are buddies. What does he say about it?"

"He doesn't say anything about it. I can't get him to talk at all about it," Tony looked down and kicked a few pebbles." That's why

I'm here. I'm hoping you'll be able to give me some insight on why he's clammed up about what happened. He used to share everything with me, but from that day on he's been as tight as a drum."

"Well, I'll tell you what I know. Maybe between the two of us we can break the logjam and get him to open up. I have to admit, he became very different after that day. Prior to it, he was very gregarious, always talking and joking with the troops. After it, he was sullen and very touchy about almost everything. People were reluctant to even talk to him." Sergeant Cole looked past Tony as if trying to see something beyond the juniper trees and yucca plants bordering the fence. When he looked back, there was a hard set to his jaw. His eyes which earlier seemed to twinkle looked like two cold gray stones. He stared at Tony for a moment, then said in a flat voice," That was a tough day. Let's go inside and I'll tell you about it."

* * * *

When they entered the house Tony was surprised by how cool the interior was. Obviously, Texans had figured out how to make their homes comfortable even in the oppressive prairie heat.

Sergeant Cole walked immediately to the refrigerator and took out two beers. He handed one to Tony and sat in an easy chair opposite him. After a long swig of his beer he said," In order to understand that day fully, we have to go back eight months earlier to when Captain Cavello took over the company." He studied the beer in his hand as he collected his thoughts about that long ago time.

Tony remained silent.

"He took over from Captain Caldwell who commanded the company for six months. Everyone liked Caldwell. He had been an enlisted man for about five years before he went to OCS and got his commission. He could really relate to the enlisted men, especially the NCOs. When we were back at the base camp he would spend more time drinking with the NCOs then he did with the officers. His Field First and he were very close. In addition, the XO, Lieutenant Sterling was an OCS grad so he and Captain Caldwell had a lot in common. Anyhow, the three of them molded every aspect of the company into a unit that reflected what they thought our company should be. It wasn't a bad company, but it also wasn't as good as it could have been. It was a pretty 'hang loose' outfit. There were very few yes sirs and no sirs and a lot of first names. I didn't agree with how the company was being run, but I was a platoon sergeant, so I just kept my mouth shut and made sure my platoon was squared away. My platoon leader was Lieutenant Hawkins, a bright young West Point officer. He used to get all sorts of flack from Captain Caldwell because the lieutenant was always trying to do things by the book. You know, immediate action drills, fire and movement, following SOPs, that kind of stuff. The old man would ride him unmercifully and tease him about being a book soldier, not a real combat soldier like he was. Unfortunately, Lieutenant Hawkins got killed shortly before Captain Covello took over. I believe he would have enjoyed serving under him.

Well, when Captain Covello took over the company it was like an earthquake hit the unit. He and Captain Caldwell couldn't have been more different. Captain Covello was all about military courtesy and protocol. He was an avid reader of every combat study he could get his hands on. I remember that he had a very worn copy of "Street Without Joy" that he kept in his pack. He would read it whenever he could, trying to learn as much as possible from the French experience.

Caldwell stayed with us for a few days to help Captain Covello with the transition. He and the XO and the Field First used to make fun of the new C.O. because of his studious approach to running a company in combat. They called him the professor. The joke they told around the company was that the definition of a professor was someone who knew how to make love 32 different ways, but didn't know any women. What they meant was that Captain Covello knew all the techniques, but didn't have any combat experience. The whole company was in on the joke.

So, when Captain Covello began to implement his policies to mold the company into what he thought a combat unit ought to be, he got some pushback. For instance, he had us work on our SOP to ensure that all units came online when one unit became engaged. We worked on wheeling right or wheeling left or coming up on either flank if the center platoon was engaged.

Well, you can imagine how well this training went over with all those combat hardened troops. Many of them had been in the field for six months or longer. They weren't going to roll over and play soldier again, especially not after six months under Caldwell. In time, Caldwell's XO and Field First and some of the guys who had been in the company the longest rotated out. Little by little the old man got the company he wanted.

He picked me to be his Field First. I'd like to say with all due to humility that I helped him a lot. There's nothing like a swift boot in the ass to help some uncommitted troop to see the wisdom of your way.

Captain Covello did a lot to help us get ready for that awful day by insisting that we use techniques that had been proven to work. And, he was creative. He sent a few NCOs to work with the Australians so that they could learn tracking techniques which they in turn taught to others in the company. He sent other NCOs to visit the Marines in I Corps so that they could learn sniper techniques which we implemented.

Nonetheless, he was the butt of many jokes, especially from the old-timers because of his persistence in getting the company to follow proper techniques," Sergeant Cole paused for a moment. He looked at Tony and said very forcefully," After that awful day, no one had anything but praise for the old man, even from the old-timers. His dogged insistence in training the company properly saved a lot of lives that day. As you know sir, once the fight starts there are no do overs.

It's a 'come as you are' battle. Thanks to him, we were as ready as we could be."

He reached over and took Tony's empty beer can and walked into the kitchen. He tossed both cans into the trash and replaced them with two fresh beers from the refrigerator. He took a long swig of his beer and then sat back down in his chair. He looked at Tony for a moment and then at nothing in particular on the opposing wall. Tony noticed that he narrowed his eyes before he spoke in a soft voice," Okay, now I'm ready to tell you about that day".

* * * *

"Avenger Six, Avenger One Six over," Marco's platoon leader of the lead platoon broke the silence .

"This is Avenger Six over," Marco answered.

"This is avenger One Six. I don't like the looks or feel of the area to our front. I am going to slow down and bring my squads online. I am also going to send a fire team forward to see what's ahead of us. Over."

"Avenger Six, Roger out."

As soon as Marco's short response ended, all hell broke loose around the first platoon's position. From the volume of fire to his front, it was obvious to Marco that his first platoon was heavily engaged.

"Avenger Six, Avenger One Six, am pinned down by at least a platoon size unit, over." The radio transmission confirmed what Marco could see and hear to his front.

"Avenger 16, Roger that. Help is on the way per our SOP, over," Marco's calm voice seemed out of place among the noise and bedlam swirling around the lead platoon.

An ominous silence greeted Marco's response. He waited a moment and then tried again to reach his platoon leader." Avenger 16, this is Avenger six over." Marco's voice had more urgency in it this time." Come in 16," Marco tried again.

After a nerve wracking delay, an unfamiliar and frantic voice responded." Avenger six, Lieutenant Blake his RTO and the platoon sergeant are all down. They' enemy is in the trees all around us. We need help," the voice pleaded.

Marco gave the handset to his RTO and moved quickly to the sounds of the gunfire. He bounded from tree to tree, seeking whatever cover was available. There was not much vegetation between the trees, so he had to survey the area carefully before making each move. As he got closer to the battle, he could hear bullets clipping the leaves above him and occasionally smacking into the tree trunks around him. He was planning his next move when he noticed Sergeant Cole waving to him from behind a tree about 50 yards in front of him. He caught his breath, then rushed in a crouch across the open area. He fell heavily next to the sergeant, half sliding and half diving into a protected position behind the same tree. Marco was panting heavily as he squirmed next to Sergeant Cole, making sure he was completely hidden by the tree. Bullets clipped the branches and leaves around him. Periodically rounds hit the trunk of the tree with a solid thunk. It was obvious to Marco that one or more snipers knew that he and Sergeant Cole were hunkered down behind the tree. He knew that any attempt to leave the cover of the tree would be very dangerous.

After he caught his breath, Marco spoke in a calm, measured voice." We need to get some artillery or mortar support as well as some gunships to help mask the movements of the second and third platoons coming on line," he seemed to be thinking through his plan out loud. The volume of fire picked up considerably. Because his own men were pinned down, Marco could tell that the heaviest fire was clearly coming from the enemy. Periodically, Marco could hear the sickening sound of bullets hitting flesh followed often by the mournful cry of 'medic' from those that had been hit. The firing hitting his men was now coming from three sides. The first platoon was strung out along a trail and was being picked to pieces by the snipers and enemy soldiers in prepared positions to the front and both flanks. Marco could tell by the frequent cries for help that the platoon was taking heavy casualties. His rage and anger continued to build as

Marco realized that his soldiers were being killed and wounded in the ambush and he was unable to do anything to stop it. He rose into a crouch preparing to leave the cover of the tree.

"Where are you going sir?" Sergeant Cole said as he pulled Marco back down roughly." Getting you killed or wounded won't help us one bit."

"I have to get to a goddamn radio before they're all killed," Marco screamed.

When Sergeant Cole pulled Marco down their faces were close together. He could see the wild look in Marco's eyes. His face was so contorted, Sergeant Cole thought for a moment he had been wounded.

Marco thrashed around trying to get free of Sergeant Cole's grip." I need a radio," he shrieked again.

"Sir, calm down. When the other two platoons come on line to the flanks like you trained them, we'll regain superiority of fire. Then you can find your RTO and get the support we need. Just give it a few minutes more," Sergeant Cole said in a soothing voice that belied his feelings of the seriousness of the situation.

Marco's heavy breathing slowly subsided. He looked at Sergeant Cole as if he were seeing him for the first time. He pulled the sergeant's hands away, releasing the tight grip that held them close together.

Sergeant Cole could see Marco's body relax. The wild look in his eyes was gone, replaced by a calm look of determination." You're right," Marco said softly.

Looking past Marco, Sergeant Cole could see Golinski, Marco's RTO half hidden behind a tree about 50 yards away."There's Golinski sir, to our right rear behind that tree."

Marco slowly shifted his body so that he could also see the RTO."Thank God!" he exclaimed when he saw him."Okay, here's what we're going to do," Marco's calm, steady voice had returned." I'll pop a blue smoke. That will do two things. Per our SOP that will alert everyone in the area who doesn't already know it, that we have snipers in the trees. It will also give Chambers a little concealment as he crosses the open area between us. When I pop the smoke you give him as much cover as you can by spraying the trees around us to keep the snipers busy."

"I got it sir. Good plan," Sergeant Cole said.

Marco squirmed closer to the tree and sat up and put his back to the trunk so that he could signal his RTO as well as to make room for him.

Golinski peeked tentatively around the tree several times before Marco caught his attention. Through a series of hand gestures he signaled the RTO that he wanted him to join him. Golinski became wide-eyed when he realized what his company commander was asking him to do. Marco held up the smoke grenade and simulated throwing it to let the scared soldier know he would try to provide concealment for him during the dash. He then pointed to Sergeant Cole and took his rifle and simulated shooting into the trees so he knew that he would also be given some covering fire.

Marco then pantomimed having a radio and pointing to the sky at the same time to let Golinski know that he wanted the radio in order to get the air support they needed.

Golinski ducked behind the tree again as bullets clipped the branches above his head. After a moment, he peeked around the the tree with a smile. He gave Marco a thumbs-up.

"Here we go," Marco said as he popped the blue smoke grenade. At the same time, Sergeant Cole began spraying the treetops around them even though he didn't have a specific target. As the blue smoke wafted around them, Marco looked expectedly at the young soldier 50 yards away. He gave a gentle wave to the RTO to give him one last bit of encouragement. At that moment their eyes locked. Marco could see the trust and respect that Golinski had as he readied to make his move. With a burst, he sprang from behind the tree and began his short dash toward Marco. He got halfway across the open area when the cord of the handset got caught on a bush. He struggled for only a moment to free the cord before a bullet smacked into his chest. The impact stood him straight up. Marco could clearly see the young man's face. He seemed to have a look of surprise as he fell over backwards. He tried to move again before two more rounds hit him. The awful sound of the thud of bullets hitting flesh carried clearly to Marco over the noise of battle. As he watched in horror, several more bullets slammed into the inert body causing it to jump slightly each time.

"Those bastards," Marco yelled as he rose to a kneeling position, preparing to run to his fallen RTO."Those bastards," he screamed again.

Sergeant Cole reached up and grabbed his web gear and pulled him down before he could leave the cover of the tree. "You can't help him now. You'll get killed if you go out there. And that won't help anyone."

"Those bastards," he hissed as he turned away from looking at the fallen soldier 25 yards away. Sergeant Cole could sense that the intensity of the fire from the first platoon was slowly increasing, especially the fire directed at the treetops. There was a corresponding slackening of the enemy's fire." I believe that your blue smoke did the trick sir," he said."At a minimum, those snipers have to be more careful with everyone watching the trees now."

"Let's see if we can get the guy that got Golinski," Marco's wild look had returned. He's got to be fairly close. I'm going to give him a glimpse of my helmet to try to determine about where he is," Marco said as he removed his helmet. He put it on a stick and nudged it just passed the trunk of the tree. He pulled it back after only a few seconds when nothing happened. He waited a few minutes and eased it out a little further this time. A bullet smacked into the tree just above the helmet as Marco pulled it back.

"He's still there," he said with a sickly grin."I want his ass. I'm going to run back to that tree that Golinski was behind. He'll be watching me. It'll take him a second to get a bead on me. That'll have to be enough time for you to locate him and get him."

"Not a good plan, sir. If I can't find him before he zeros in on you, you're a dead man. We'll get him in due time," the sergeant answered.

"He's not expecting me to go back the way I came. He's expecting us to stay behind this tree. I'm fast enough that'll it'll take him a second or two to adjust to my zigzag movements back to that tree. That will be your chance. End of discussion," Marco said as he adjusted his position so that he would be able to spring quickly from behind the tree." You ready Sergeant Cole?"

Without waiting for an answer, Marco sprang from behind the tree, running rapidly toward his destination 50 yards to the rear. Sergeant Cole rolled left of the tree, exposing as little of himself as he could. He anxiously scanned the trees to his front frantically trying to see some movement that would reveal the sniper's position. He knew that every second counted. He panicked when he initially couldn't detect any movement. He heard a shot fired above him and further to the right then he had been looking. It was then that he saw a figure, cleverly camouflaged with palm fronds in a tree 30 yards away. He hoped that the round just fired hadn't hit Marco. He took a deep breath while sighting on the semi hidden figure. With a gentle squeeze he fired off three short bursts at the sniper. He was about to fire another burst, when he saw the enemy straighten up and fall heavily to the ground.

Sergeant Cole ducked back behind the tree, trembling as he resumed his hidden position. He frantically searched the trees behind him before he saw Marco. He stuck his head out for a moment and gave the sergeant a thumbs up.

* * * *

Sergeant Cole gripped his beer with two hands and looked at Tony for a moment." The way I figure it, it was a win-win for the old man. If I got the sniper first, Chambers got his revenge. If the sniper got Captain Covello first he wouldn't be haunted any more by that awful day". He paused for a long moment, "If you ask me, the old man was rooting for the sniper." He looked out the window for a few minutes as if trying to remember something he had forgotten.

When he looked back at Tony, he was smiling." What the old man forgot was that I am an excellent shot. That's how his plan got screwed up."

Tony looked at the tough old soldier for a moment."Wow! Thank you so much Sergeant Cole. You filled in a whole lot of blanks that help me to understand what happened to my buddy."

"Captain Covello was never the same after that day," Sergeant Cole continued after a long swig of his beer.

"How did you guys finally overcome the ambush?" Tony asked.

"Well, it was pretty anti-climatic. Our two other platoons came up on line and we established fire superiority just the way Captain Covello had trained us. He got a radio from one of the platoon leaders and got us some gunship support and later some fast movers to pound the area to our front. We finally got some artillery support after we had pretty much secured the area. Charlie Company finally linked up with us late in the afternoon. It was close to dusk by the time we got our wounded and dead out and got resupplied so we set out some LPs and dug in for the night. It had been a long hard day so we were content to just hunker down and wait for any possible counterattack."

"What did the battalion commander say about that?" Tony moved to the edge of his chair to hear the answer.

"Oh, he was ranting and raving about us moving out of there, but the old man was adamant about staying put to make sure we got all our wounded out. As I said, by the time we finished evacuating the wounded it was almost dark. The aviation guys weren't so thrilled about flying in the dark, so they took the Colonel back to the base camp and we got some peace and quiet."

"Did Captain Covello ever mentioned that kid again, his RTO?"

"He mentioned him only once to me after that day. It was at the memorial service we had for our KIAs a few weeks later back at the base camp. We were standing together while Father Muldoon conducted the service. Captain Covello looked awful. I'll never forget it. His complexion was almost gray and his eyes had a far away, haunted look. I thought there was something wrong with him, but he wouldn't go and have the doc check him out. Anyhow, during the service he looked at me with those weary, haunted eyes and said in a barely audible hoarse voice, "That boy trusted me and it got him killed. I'll never forget the look in his eyes just before he tried to reach me." I never heard him mention Chambers again. I do know that he wrote a letter to the boy's parents back in Detroit. I know he agonized over that letter for a long time because I saw him in his tent just staring off into the distance with the pen in his hand for several nights. Emory, the company clerk gave me a heads up when the old man finally gave him the letter to mail."

"I know how hard it is to write those letters. I had to write a few of them myself. I remember thinking that I could never express myself well enough to comfort a grieving mother or father. There just aren't any words that can comfort a mother who raised that boy and sat with him when he was sick and who had such hopes and aspirations for him. I've never felt so inadequate in my entire life as when I had to write those letters".

They both sat silently for a moment as the room darkened matching their gloomy mood. Finally, Sergeant Cole walked over to a lamp and turned it on. "One more thing I think you should understand about the old man and that day. He was burned out. We all knew it. He had been in the field almost nonstop for almost 8 months before that operation. He had an R and R, but he came back early because he found out that company had taken casualties while he was gone.

You know in World War II they learned that infantry troops became ineffective if they were left in the front line for over 90 days. Our combat wasn't as intense as World War II, but the concept still applies. For the old man, I believe staying in the field for the better part of eight months finally got to him on that day. There was no front line, but every day and every night held the possibility of combat. And that required a constant state of vigilance. I could see that he took every casualty we had in the company personally. He was always trying to figure out what he could have or should have done differently after our firefights, especially those where we had casualties. I could see the pressure building in him. I even spoke to the Battalion Sergeant Major about it. I know he went to Colonel Braddock, our old Battalion CO. I believe Braddock was about to recommend that Captain Covello be brought in from the field and replace him just before the Colonel rotated out. That new battalion commander Cooper, was a boob. He didn't care about anyone other than himself. So, the old man stayed in the field just a little too long. Most company commanders were replaced after six months in the field. Captain Covello was way overdue," Sergeant Cole looked down at his clenched hands, clearly frustrated by the retelling of the story.

"I believe you're right Sergeant Cole. All of the other company commanders of the battalion got rotated out. Captain Covello resisted every effort to get him to give up the company. When I asked him why, he said he couldn't let the men of the company down by leaving them. He felt no one else could or would take care of them like he would. He should have been ordered to relinquish command, but the change of battalion commander's messed that up," Tony said as he moved to the edge of his chair.

They were both silent for a moment. Finally, Sergeant Cole looked up. There was sadness in his eyes."You know, some guys never left Viet Nam completely. Captain Covello is one of those guys. What can we do to bring him home?"

Tony reached across and gave Sergeant Cole's clenched hands a gentle squeeze. That gesture spoke volumes to the two old comrades in arms. They both smiled in recognition of the bond they shared." I'm working on it. That's what this whole trip is about. I'm trying to get Captain Covello to come to terms with not only that day, but his complete tour in Vietnam. He's a tough nut to crack. It may take some time but I know I'll wear him down."

"Well, you can try that touchy-feely, officer stuff. Or, you can use the same technique that NCOs used in airborne school when someone had an emotional problem. They tell them just to suck it up. I had some buddies like Captain Covello and it was the tough love approach that finally got them to snap out of it.

"I am going to try the touchy-feely officer stuff as you call it, first. If that doesn't work I may call on you to deliver the less subtle drill sergeant technique," Tony said as they both laughed.

* * * *

After a quick supper of chicken fried steak and french fries at the town's only restaurant, Tony and Sergeant Cole said their goodbyes.

"Keep me posted on your progress on the old man and that dumb match you set up sir. If you ask me, a little meeting behind your office building would have been a better way to teach that draft dodger to show some respect for our efforts, " Sergeant Cole said with a laugh.

"You're probably right Top, but in New Jersey they don't understand the Texas method of resolving differences. We have to be a little more subtle up there," Tony said with a grin.

They looked at each other for a moment, then embraced in a big bear hug."Welcome home," they both said simultaneously.

"I'll be in touch," Tony said as he got in his car.

Sergeant Cole snapped a salute once Tony got settled behind the wheel. Tony returned the salute and said," The little guy doesn't stand a chance with you and I both on the case." As Tony pulled away, he looked in his rearview mirror and saw that Sergeant Cole remained in a ramrod position of attention until he couldn't see him any longer.

CHAPTER SIXTEEN

A FOND FAREWELL

They had planned to leave before dawn for the trip back to the East Coast. Tony and Marco would be flying back to give Marco a chance to rest up and overcome any jet lag before the match. The others would drive continuously, planning to arrive the night before the match. The night before they were to leave, Rudy asked them to delay their departure long enough to have breakfast with him the following morning.

It was just after six in the morning as Tony drove on to the grounds of the tennis club

"Lucky I changed my mind about taking home a souvenir. I was going to buy an ashtray, but there's no room in this van," Freddy observed."Have you ever noticed that suitcases always swell to three times their original size on a return trip?"

"Have you ever noticed that philosophy and 6 o'clock in the morning don't go together," Tony yawned.

Only Marco seemed fully awake. The others were trying to recover from an almost all night farewell to Dallas." Okay you guys, rise and shine, we're almost here and I think you all should be semiconscious to thank Rudy. He did an awful lot for all of us," Marco said seriously.

"Sure, listen to Mr. Morning Glory. You did nothing but live cleanly and sleep for two weeks. We had to uphold the dignity and reputation of Ranger manhood that whole time. We're exhausted," Chuck said.

"Well, whatever your sacrifices, and I'm sure they were great, we owe it to Rudy to be awake and civil," Marco replied.

"Marco's right boys. Rise and shine. You guys driving back have three days to sleep," Tony added.

The clubhouse had no visible activity as they pulled up to the entrance."Rudy said the front door would be open and we should meet him in his executive dining room," Marco informed his friends.

After leaving the van, they entered the building and made their way down the empty corridors." Boy, it seems like only yesterday we were dodging Biff and Miss German Shepherd at the front desk. Now here we are having breakfast with the big guy in his private dining room," Tony remarked proudly.

"Well, it might seem like only yesterday for you, but I feel like I'm wrapping up a ten year sentence of hard labor," Marco added sarcastically.

"Holy mackerel, right on time," Rudy greeted them outside of the dining room." But then you guys are used to early reveilles aren't you?"

"No problem for us," Freddy lied.

"I hope this wasn't too much of an inconvenience for you. I know you wanted to get off early so we'll make this as quick as possible. I just wanted to say goodbye to all of you together. But first, I wanted to make you sure you all had a good meal before starting your trip"

"Did our mothers call you Rudy?" Tony asked with a grin as they entered the dining room.

* * * *

"Wow, I'm absolutely stuffed," Tony said, wiping his mouth.

"It's a good thing Marco and I are flying back because I don't believe we all could fit back in that van right now."

"I know what you mean Tony. It's a good thing we didn't eat this much while we were in the van, they would have had to use a giant can opener to get us out," Chuck added.

Listen, I asked you all to stop in for more than just fattening you up. I wanted to tell you how important these last two weeks have been for me," Rudy said seriously. The room became silent as Rudy continued. "I don't know if Tony told you that my son was an Air Force pilot in Vietnam. He was shot down over the North in 1968 and has been missing ever since. Having you here these last two weeks reminded me of what it was like when Rudy and his friends used to visit. It was one huge goat rodeo from dawn to dusk." Everyone smiled at Rudy's descriptive phrase.

"Well, I'd hoped I'd have been able to welcome him home but the Lord decided otherwise. These last two weeks have helped to give me some peace about knowing I can never hold him and say 'Welcome Home'. However, I would very much like very much to say to all of you with great affection,'Welcome Home.'"

Rudy sat down. The room became completely silent. All of the others in the room stared at their plates, not daring to look up for fear that they would show the emotion which had grabbed them following Rudy's farewell. Tony was the first to move. He walked over to Rudy who rose to meet him. They embraced for a moment." You know, I thought getting Marco ready for this big match and your hospitality was a great gift for all of us. And as wonderful as that was, your 'Welcome Home' is what we'll most remember about our wonderful two weeks with you," he said.

Each of the others in the room got up and embraced the smiling tennis pro. Marco was the last to approach Rudy. "Coach, I don't know how to thank you for all you've done," he said.

"You can thank me best by beating the pants off that wimp who challenged you. When Tony first approached me about this whole cockamamie scheme, I thought he had really exaggerated the whole thing."

"Who me exaggerate?" Tony yelled from across the room to the guffaws of his friends.

"But you know what?" Rudy continued with a broader smile." I believe Tony's right. It's a battle between good and evil. "The group erupted in applause and hoots, spurring Rudy on. "The fate of Western Civilization may be determined by the outcome of this match." There was more laughter, applause and hoots. "And most important of all," Rudy continued," We all get a chance to destroy a pompous asshole." Everyone rushed to Rudy and Marco and embraced them both in an enormous huddle.

CHAPTER SEVENTEEN

KATHY

Kathy knocked gently on the door. After a short time, she could hear movement in the house and then the porch light came on." Kathy what are you doing here?" Tony asked as he opened the door.

"I just stopped by to wish the champ good luck before the big match tomorrow night."

"Well come right on in. This is great! The Fair Lady Kathy visits her champion before the trial of combat. I hope you brought a scarf or something he can wear during the match," Tony said with a sweeping bow.

"Boy, Marco's right. You are the master of the melodramatic. You make Hans Christian Andersen look like he had no imagination at all," Kathy said curtsying before entering the house." Where is Sir Marco?"

"I'm really glad you came tonight. I was just leaving to go see my West Point roommate. Sit here for a moment while I explain what's going on." Tony pointed to the sofa while he sat down in a nearby chair.

"Right now he's up in his room. I hope he's getting psyched for the match. Actually, I'm very glad you're here because I know he's up there listening to World War II music. He does this about once every six months. He goes off by himself, puts on all that old music and loses himself in his own thoughts. He tries to pretend I don't know what he's thinking about, but I know. However, he's made it clear to me that he really wants me to leave him alone during these periods, so I do." Tony said, looking away from Kathy for a moment.

When he looked back at her, Kathy could see sadness in his eyes. " I believe it would help our chances tomorrow night if you tried to get to him before he sinks too deeply into his semi annual mood."

"What is it that he thinks of during these times?" Kathy asked quietly.

"He'd kill me if he knew I told you, but I think you care enough about him to know. Besides, I'm hoping he trusts you enough so that maybe he'll let you help him. These sessions are getting a little more frequent and a little deeper each time."

Kathy had never seen Tony so serious. She waited quietly for him to continue.

Tony looked away again and stared vacantly out of the window for a moment. When he looked back Kathy could see that his eyes had welled up with tears.

"What is it Tony?" Kathy asked moving to the edge of the sofa and gently touching Tony's hand.

Tony gave a little sigh, then answered, " You know Marco and I were company commanders in Vietnam. Towards the end of our tour in November, the month before we came home, our battalion was sent on a mission close to the Cambodian border. Until that time we had been in a number of fire fights. During all of those other actions Marco's company had hardly any casualties. After eight months as a company commander and in fairly heavy contact he had only 10 people killed and a few more wounded. All of the other companies, including the one I later commanded, had much higher casualties. It was the damnedest thing. People started to say that Marco was the good luck charm for his troops and as long as he was with them, nobody would get hurt. As a matter of fact, seven of the KIAs in his company happened when he was on R&R.

Marco was a good officer, one of the best. But no one can really protect folks once you get into a fight. Well, the legend started to build. Everyone wanted to believe it. I could see the pressure it was putting on Marco, so I pooh-poohed it every time I heard it. It was kind of like reminding a pitcher every inning that he has a no-hitter going. Marco became downright violent whenever anyone mentioned it to him. I think you can guess what happened. Marco's company was the lead company for a battalion search and destroy mission.

We had all three of our infantry companies, two Vietnamese companies and our reconnaissance platoon on the operation. The battalion was all spread out. It was a bad plan from the beginning. We were all supposed to converge on a North Vietnamese concentration of troops from different directions. Marco's company ran into the enemy first. The bad guys let about half of Marco's company pass before they pinned them down and started to work them over with snipers. Most of the ARVN left, leaving Marco's company way out and isolated. He did everything he could to disengage and withdraw, but he couldn't. They pounded him all afternoon. It wasn't until almost nightfall that Marco was able to call in enough artillery and air support to force the North Vietnamese to withdraw. By the time we were able to link up with him and his troops, Marco had lost 20 men killed and 40 wounded. That was almost 50% of his company.

Well, you can imagine what that did to Marco. There was nothing he could do about it. He did everything he could. He was moving constantly throughout his company, redistributing ammunition, shifting his men and tending to the wounded. His company beat off a number of NVA attempts to overrun his position. I believe Marco was the major reason why there weren't many more casualties. He was ordered several times to withdraw, but he wouldn't leave his dead and wounded." Tony got up and began to pace the room.

"One of the other companies finally reached Marco and his men late in the day. By then, the main enemy force had left. There were only a few snipers left in the area. I'm told that Marco was like a maniac, he was almost incoherent. He kept saying over and over again that it was his fault, that he should've known that the North Vietnamese were there. Well, our whole battalion got fooled, so it wasn't his fault at all. As a matter of fact, Marco got the Distinguished Service Cross, the second highest award for valor the army gives out.

When the relief force pushed past Marco's Company to clear the area, they found over 70 dead North Vietnamese. He couldn't have done more, nobody could have. But Marco has always felt that it was his fault. He changed from that day. He used to joke and fool around as much as I do. Every once in a while, I can see the old spark again, but then something seems to go off inside him. It's almost as if it's reminding him that he shouldn't be happy."

"You know Tony, I've always felt there was something buried inside of Marco. The closer I got, the more apparent it became. Thank you so much for sharing this with me. You'll never know how grateful I am. It may just be girlish optimism, but I think I can help. A couple of times it almost seemed that Marco was reaching out for me to help him. I never knew for sure so I never knew what to do," Kathy said.

"I sure hope you can help Kathy. I believe our little cross country trip may have stirred up the memories again. We passed near where some of his old company members live and I tried to get Marco to visit, or at least call them. He wouldn't have any part of it. Most of his guys have tried to write to him or call him over the years since they came home. I've spoken to them when Marco wouldn't. They think Marco's a hero. They really believe that it was his actions that prevented their position from being overrun and all of them from being killed. Most of them were wounded so they wouldn't have been able to move if they had been forced to withdraw," Tony added.

"I would have never guessed any of this Tony," Kathy said seriously."Marco never mentioned Vietnam to me. He seems so gentle, it's hard to believe he went through all of that."

"I believe that contrast exists in all men who have been in combat. I've always said that war brings out the best and worst of the human spirit. We go around trying to kill other human beings, the absolute worst of all human endeavors. However, I believe because of the unnatural horror of war, most soldiers somehow sense that they have to balance the ledger for their own sanity by expressing greater love for their fellow soldiers. I can't tell you the number of times I've seen guys risk their lives, and sometimes give them up in an attempt to help their buddies. No one is very showy about it, but you're so close you just sense that your buddies will be there if you need them. I once heard that the ancient Greeks had three words for love. One was to describe the love of a mother for a child, another to describe the love between a man and woman and the third to describe the love that soldiers feel for each other. I don't know if the story about the Greeks is true, but I sure saw lots of examples of that third kind of love when I was in Vietnam.

That's why I need your help in assisting Marco to face this problem. He needs to balance his ledger by acknowledging the love he and his troops share. He's turned away from it because he feels responsible for what happened, and he's left with only the horror."

Kathy got up and gently kissed Tony on the cheek. You know, I've learned a lot about both you and Marco tonight. There are a lot of similarities between you. That's probably why you're both such good friends. You both have this façade which masks how deep and profound you both are. I believe facing death at an early age probably has made you older than your years,"

"Hey, wait a minute doctor. The patient is upstairs.," Tony said hugging Kathy.

"I understand Tony," Kathy said gently.

"You know, I think you do understand. And not many people do. I kind of gave my little speech to you because I sensed that you would understand. I've never really shared that much with anyone else before. Thanks," Tony said with a smile.

Kathy kissed him again on the cheek."Thank you," she said softly.

"Okay, time to go to work doctor," Tony said enthusiastically, changing the mood." The real challenge is one flight up, immersed by now probably in the mood and music of about 1944. Your mission, should you accept it, is to bring him safely back to 1992."

"I accept and I believe I can do it. How about another hug for good luck though," Kathy said.

"You've got it. I would do anything for Marco, even if it means I have to hug a beautiful woman," Tony said with a grin.

"Well, I'm off to see my old West Point roommate, Bill. I like to keep him in the loop. I want to tell him about our trip and Marco's big match. We have great conversations, Bill and me. You take care of Marco. Tell him I'll be back a little after midnight."

They embraced for a moment. Kathy left the room and walked to the stairway. She could hear music coming from the second floor. She walked slowly up the stairs thinking about all she had just learned from Tony. By the time she got to Marco's door, she was less certain about what she'd say or do or how he might react to her intrusion. She took a deep breath and knocked gently on the door.

"Who is it?" The voice sounded alarmed.

Kathy could tell it was Marco, but he sounded very subdued, almost like a child."It's me, Kathy," she said opening the door at the same time. Marco was sitting across the room in an easy chair. He didn't make an attempt to get up. Although she had been anticipating this moment, the shock of it still overwhelmed her. *There's real sadness in this room*, she thought. *I can actually feel it.* It reminded her of the time when she was a little girl and visited her grandmother after her grandfather had died. She remembered that she could feel that total sadness and grief were present.

"Marco, I just came by to wish you good luck before the big match tomorrow night," Kathy stammered. *Dammit I wanted to be so sure and positive about this and I'm all flustered,* she thought to herself. She moved quickly across the room to Marco, gaining a little confidence as she approached him." What's wrong Marco. You look so sad, " Kathy said gently.

Marco looked at her for a moment, then looked away without speaking.

"Marco whatever burden you are carrying is too much for one human being. Let me help you. I want to share whatever problems you have," Kathy said as she sat on the arm of the chair next to him. She gently pulled his head to her and started to stroke his hair." It's okay Marco. I can help. Trust me. You need to trust someone. You can't hold it inside anymore. Tell me, what is it?"

Marco didn't move for a moment. He let Kathy hold him and continue to stroke his hair. After a short time, he took a deep breath. His entire body trembled for a second. He pulled away from Kathy and looked at her. She thought she had never seen a sadder human being. She could feel her own heart grow heavy and overcome with sorrow as if there were too much sadness in the room to be borne only by Marco.

"Oh Kathy," Marco groaned." It was my fault. I should've known they were there. I should have halted the company and scouted ahead. They waited until we got so close that we didn't have a chance." The words were tumbling out now in disconnected sentences." It was my fault. They would all still be alive today if I hadn't been in such a hurry. Then, when we got trapped, nobody came. We couldn't move and nobody came to help us. I tried to get the wounded behind cover, but the North Vietnamese kept changing positions and shooting them. I saw someone drag Sergeant Miller behind a big ant hill, but he fell over and they shot him again. Barnes, he was only 18, got shot in the stomach and couldn't control himself. He died in his own excrement, calling for his mother. Oh Kathy it was awful. It went on all day. We couldn't get out of there." Marco buried his head in his hands. He trembled again, pulled away and took a deep breath.

"You know what" he said looking at her." I'm so sad, but I've never been able to cry. My heart is so heavy sometimes I think it's going to stop because it's truly broken. But I've never been able to cry. I don't understand that. I want to cry, but I can't. I didn't cry when it happened that day and I haven't been able to cry since then, no matter how much I think about it."

"It doesn't matter Marco. You did everything you could. You have to give up the guilt. You'll torture yourself if you keep trying to relive that day. You're the only one blaming you. The army cited you for bravery and your own company mates think you were magnificent and saved lives. You're just too emotional about the whole thing to make a rational decision about it. You did what you could for those who died. You can't bring them back. You have an obligation to the living now. A lot of us need you Marco. Don't let us down by living in the past," Kathy said with a sob. "Hold me, just told me."

He held her tightly, then began stroking her hair gently." It's okay Kathy. Thank you. I'll be okay. Just stay here with me for a little while."

CHAPTER EIGHTEEN

BILL

As Tony reached the northern part of the Garden State Parkway, the traffic thinned considerably. He opened the window slightly to let the cool night air engulf him. He kept the radio off. The only noises he could hear were the hum of his own tires and the sound of occasional trucks as he passed them. Here and there, lights twinkled warmly in the gathering darkness of this sparsely populated area of northern New Jersey.

Tony had made this trip alone many times since 1966. He welcomed the solitude and silence of the journey. It allowed him to recall vividly the times that he and Bill had returned to West Point together along this same route after weekend leaves. He treasured rides like this one tonight back to the Academy because they brought him closer to Bill and the memories they had shared.

Bill had grown up in Indiana and was uninterested in the east coast until he met Barbara. Tony smiled as he recalled again how he had been instrumental in getting Bill and Barbara together. It happened on a warm spring Saturday at West Point toward the end of their plebe year.

* * * *

1958

"Okay boys, these are sophisticated and pure New Jersey women. Do not embarrass me by attempting to force your crude and boorish midwestern or southern behavior on these ladies. They have been raised surrounded by charming, sophisticated and erudite men like me, so your bumpkin charm will be ineffective."

Tony's proclamation was met by boos and hisses.

"And, be especially respectful to those ladies whose names may end in a vowel," Tony continued ignoring the reaction of his classmates." Unless you want to meet up with the uncle Guido or the Uncle Bruno of these Italian-American princesses, you better be on your best behavior."

"Tell me Tony, how did a guy like you who has barely had a date during plebe year, all of a sudden find fifteen women willing to travel to West Point to meet us fifteen cloistered men?" John asked to an accompaniment of more hoots and guffaws from the group.

"Oh ye of little faith and gratitude. Here I am risking my reputation in New Jersey to give you monk-like recluses a chance to share some female companionship and I'm met with derision. How ungrateful."

Just then, Tony spotted Brenda striding resolutely up to the hostess' desk followed closely by 14 of her less certain companions. Without another word to his friends, Tony walked quickly toward Brenda and greeted her enthusiastically with a handshake. He knew better than to give a hug to his old high school friend in this very public place. Public displays of affection beyond the handshake, even for old friends, was strictly forbidden. Tony knew that any PDA observed by the hostess or an officer would result in the offender receiving five demerits.

The only place at the academy where holding hands was permitted was Flirtation Walk. Even there, physical contact between couples was limited by the large number of other cadets and their dates who populated the winding and scenic trails along the banks of the Hudson river.

After brief introductions, the cadets and women accompanying Brenda paired off and scattered to various sporting events or other activities on the campus.

At the end of the day, they all reassembled at Grant Hall to say goodbye. Tony noted that it appeared that none of the couples, including Bill and Barbara, seemed to have any interest in maintaining contact. There were cordial handshakes between the men and women, but it was obvious that both groups were anxious to return to their own activities.

It was only by coincidence months later that Tony learned that Bill and Barbara had been corresponding and talking to one another secretly since their first meeting. Their romance moved quickly after that from regular dating to engagement and marriage after Bill graduated.

* * * *

The rhythm of the sounds of the car and the loneliness of the ride seem to coax the memories easily out of Tony. He remembered fondly the four uncomplicated years he had spent at West Point, years enriched by his friendships with so many good men, especially Bill.

Bill and he had been so different. West Point had brought them together from different backgrounds and different parts of the country. Their differences faded as the academy system took hold, molding them both into future army officers. In the beginning, however, the disparity in their personalities and backgrounds made them unlikely friends.

Bill was older, almost 22, barely under the age which still made him eligible for an appointment to the Military Academy. He had worked in a steel mill in northwest Indiana before joining the army as an enlisted man. His experience made him more mature than his years. His public demeanor was very somber, intimidating to most people including the upperclassmen. During plebe year, they often passed by Bill on their way to harass easier freshmen targets such as Tony.

Tony had entered West Point right out of high school. He was barely eighteen when he stepped on to the campus to begin his cadet career. No one in his family had ever served in the military, probably since Roman times. That was evident to the upperclassmen who constantly found uniform infractions whenever Tony was forced to leave the safety of his room. He used his constant joking as a defense mechanism to mask the pressure he felt in trying to cope with the rigors of a first-year cadet. Those who didn't take the time to understand Tony, thought his joking simply revealed his immaturity.

But, Bill saw through Tony's façade from the beginning. He sensed both the stresses that Tony imposed upon himself as well as the sincerity and conviction he applied to trying to be a good cadet.

When they were in their room together, away from the harassment of the upperclassmen, Bill would uncharacteristically encourage Tony in his silliest antics. It was apparent that they both welcomed the relief that such antics provided from the challenging and rigorous schedule that was imposed on all first-year cadets.

* * * *

The car glided swiftly through the darkness as Tony crossed the border into New York state. The traffic was almost nonexistent at this hour. The twinkling lights of homes became further apart giving way to the wooded rolling hills of the New Jersey, New York border region. Tony remembered that it was at this point of their journey back to the Academy, that Bill and he both would begin to shift their thoughts from the pleasant weekend they had just completed to a more concentrated focus on the assignments and challenges they knew awaited them at West Point. The banter and laughter gave way to an almost brooding silence, as they both geared up for another week of academic and military tasks that awaited them.

As their time at the academy drew to a close, these trips took on a more serious tone as they both contemplated leaving their cloistered life as cadets at West Point and becoming officers in the U.S. Army. The questions of their branch selection and schooling as well as initial duty stations crept into their discussions more frequently.

As the miles passed swiftly, Tony recalled those conversations which had held uncertainty for them as well as hope and excitement as both men contemplated the significant change they were soon to experience." The biggest demotion you'll ever receive is when you go from a cadet at West Point to Second Lieutenant in the Army," some wise grad had once told him. Now, he and Bill were about to make that same change after four years of arduous training and preparation.

Tony recalled many of those earnest and naïve discussions that Bill and he had shared on this very same ride only a few years earlier. In retrospect, Tony saw that they were naïve because they were unable to see the impact of the event which would alter their lives, the distant and faint rumblings of the war in Vietnam. *'Maybe it was better that way,'* Tony thought. Soon enough the war would become the central factor of their lives.

With a start, Tony was shaken from his reverie by seeing the exit for West Point. He sat up straighter as he looked for the familiar landmarks that would guide him through the town of Highland Falls to the Academy. On past trips he sometimes stopped at one of the restaurants or bars that lined the street leading to the Military Academy. Even though he hadn't eaten since breakfast, he wasn't hungry and had no desire to stop now. He was anxious to get to his destination and tell Bill what was going on.

He slowed as he approached the main gate to West Point. Off to his right, he could see the outline of the Thayer hotel looming over the entrance to the Academy. As he got closer to the small guardhouse at the entryway, a military policeman stepped out and moved to the side of Tony's vehicle. Tony had a smile and his ID ready.

"Good evening sir. What's your business at the Academy this evening?" He asked after Tony rolled down his window.

"I'm a grad, here to visit one of my classmates," Tony said handing over his driver's license and an identification card noting that he was indeed an alumnus of West Point.

The MP checked Tony's ID with a small flashlight. After handing back the cards, he stepped smartly back from the vehicle and saluted. "Welcome back sir," he said as Tony returned the salute.

He drove slowly along Thayer Road bordered on his right by the darkness he knew was the Hudson River. Distant lights delineated the far bank of the river. The quarters of Field grade officers on his left hand side, overlooked the roadway.

Tony always had mixed emotions when he returned to West Point. He had pleasant and vivid memories of the times he had shared with Bill and his other friends. Yet, so much had changed since his cadet days. It was difficult now to imagine that he had spent four years on these grounds. Tony rolled down both front windows, anxious to see and hear everything around him. The cool night air caused him to be keenly aware of the sights and sounds of the Academy at night. He saw only a few people walking on the pavement bordering the road. On weekends, these same walkways would be filled with cadets and their dates walking to and from the Thayer Hotel.

The broad expanse of The Plain opened up before him. As he followed the road around the parade ground, he could see the tall granite column of Trophy Point called Battle Monument. Tony knew the column was dedicated to the over 2000 regular army officers and enlisted men who had died fighting for the Union during the Civil War. He smiled as he remembered that the column was known by the northern cadets as the Civil War Monument and to the southern cadets as the monument to southern marksmanship.

Tony was glad that the hostility and animosity that had gripped West Point just prior to the Civil War, had long faded by the time he got here 100 years later.

Once past Trophy Point, the road again became bordered by the quarters of the senior officers of the Academy. After a short distance, Tony's destination lay ahead, a dark area away from the lights of the homes on the other side of the street.

He stopped the car in a small parking area bordered by a low stone wall. The mist off the river had changed to a light drizzle. Tony turned off the headlights and sat in the darkness for a moment. This was part of the ritual Tony followed before he met with his roommate. He always took this quiet time for reflection right before going to meet with Bill.

He stepped out of the car and grabbed his raincoat from the backseat. The cold drizzle felt good on his face after the long, stuffy ride. *This is a familiar home-coming to West Point in November*, he thought as he pulled the raincoat collar around his face. The weather at the academy from October to March was always marked by cold precipitation, first rain then snow. The months after Christmas leave were called Gloom Period by the cadets, an apt description Tony thought as he buttoned his raincoat. He recalled with a smile that some long ago cadet described the awful winter weather by declaring, 'If God wanted to give the world an enema, he would put it right here in the Hudson river.'

Tony made his way through an opening in the stone wall to a gravel path, barely visible in the dim light. As his eyes became accustomed to the darkness, he could make out the tombstones on either side of the path. Whenever he visited Bill here, Tony felt as if he were walking through history. The grave sites near the entrance contained veterans of the Revolutionary war and the war of 1812. Graduates of more recent wars were interred toward the back of the cemetery. That's where Bill was.

He passed many rows of markers commemorating all of America's wars and West Point's sacrifice and commitment to the country's defense. Tony followed the path he knew so well now. Even in the darkness he could find his way to Bill's final resting place. He took a deep breath as he recalled that this new section was filled now with the remains of his classmates and others who had made the ultimate sacrifice in Vietnam.

The silence was broken only by his footsteps making a crunching sound on the gravel path. As he approached Bill's grave, he said softly,"Hi Bill. I was on a little trip and I came by to tell you I missed you and wanted to fill you in on what's going on." He picked up a small stone and placed it reverently on the tombstone, aligning it with the other stones already there. He stood silently for a moment looking at the marker and its simple inscription, "Pray for Peace." His too short life was delineated by the dates carved in the monument, November 15, 1937-February 14, 1966.

He stepped back and said," I wish you were here to enjoy this, old friend. You always enjoyed a good prank especially when it brought some pompous ass down a few pegs. Marco and I.... you remember Marco the guy I served with in Vietnam. Well, Marco and I...... okay you're right, mostly I arranged this tennis match with this arrogant jerk. It's really going to be a hoot. I wish you could see it." He paused for a moment, and smiled." Who knows, maybe you will see it. I never know your schedule until you show up. I'll know if you're there," he said as he stepped forward and rearranged the stones on the marker again. When he stepped back, there were tears in his eyes." I can't tell you how much I miss you Bud, but you know. I wish so much that we could share these times together now. His shoulders shook with an involuntary sob. He wiped his eyes and said," Rest peacefully old friend. I'll be back to tell you how it all turned out." He turned, pulling the collar of his raincoat around his face again as he quickly retraced his steps out of the cemetery.

CHAPTER NINETEEN

THE MATCH

Tony and Marco entered the tennis club by a side entrance. Tony thought it best to get Marco into the dressing room without letting him see the crowd." We'll just slip in here without anyone noticing so you can get ready without any interruptions or commotion," Tony said as he guided Marco into the locker room.

"This is great. The king of commotion and chaos is all of a sudden interested in peace and quiet. You are indeed a piece of work Tony. You set up this circus and now you're interested in making sure I have peace and quiet while I'm dressing," Marco said as he slowed down to look at his friend.

Tony gave him a gentle but firm push into the locker room." Even man-of-war had to be coaxed into the starting gate," he said. He then guided Marco to a remote section of the dressing area. He removed the bag from his own shoulder and dropped it heavily on the bench in front of the locker Marco had chosen.

"Okay Marco, tonight's the payoff for all those hard days of training we had. Tonight will make it all worthwhile," Tony said as he opened a locker.

"Wait a second let me get this straight. *We* had hard days of training? As I remember, *I* was the one sweating my ass off while you were sitting around the pool with some of the most beautiful women in Texas," Marco scoffed.

"A minor point. I was on the courts with you in spirit. Besides, there was no need for both of us to kill ourselves and get all sweaty. I have to stay fresh to plan the strategy and outsmart that sleazebag, Barrington. My brains and your brawn are an unbeatable combination," Tony said with a grin.

"Yeah, well if it weren't for your brain and your mouth, I could be home relaxing instead of getting ready to make a fool of myself in front of several hundred people," Marco retorted.

"Marco, Marco. How can you be so ungrateful? Until this challenge, you were an obscure, data processing manager. You're a celebrity now with a chance to become famous. At a minimum, you have a chance to cut El Waspo Grande down to size for a lot of people, to say nothing of restoring your honor. And, I won't even mention the probable effect on the Fair Lady, Kathy."

"Those are certainly important objectives. I just wish we could have found another way to accomplish them other than going through with this absurd spectacle."

"I'll bet The Great Umberto never questioned P.T. Barnum's plans," Tony mumbled.

"What did you say?" Marco asked sharply.

"I said I bet we have a good plan," Tony lied. "Listen Marco, Barrington is in the locker room next door gloating and planning his victory party. No one knows we went to Texas for a crash course in tennis. He thinks you skipped town for a few weeks because you were scared. He's even more arrogant than he was the day you almost ripped out his throat, if you can believe that. So let's go over our plan again. Remember, beating him is only part of the mission tonight. We have to do it in such a resounding way that it gets through even Barrington's colossal ego," Tony emphasized.

Marco grunted as he began to change.

"You get suited up pal. I'm going to check the courts," Tony said as he slapped Marco on the back. He then made his way to the other end of the locker room which opened on to the tennis courts. He could hear the buzz of the audience as he approached the door. The volume of the crowd noise surprised him. When he opened the door, he stepped back, completely overwhelmed by the size of the crowd. The bleachers which had been erected on both sides of the court were filled to capacity. He made his way slowly and cautiously through the bleachers to the court. When he emerged onto the court, the crowd recognized him and let out a loud roar, followed by a chant, low at first. Soon everyone in the audience picked up the rhythmic cheer, 'Ton-ee,

Ton-ee.'

Tony was stunned by the size and enthusiasm of the crowd. His first thought was that Marco would be spooked by the reception he was likely to get which would certainly be louder and more boisterous then what Tony had just received. He stepped tentatively on to the court and waved to the crowd, hoping that would lower the noise. Instead, the audience erupted with a louder and more raucous rendition of the chant, 'Ton-ee, Ton-ee.'

Tony waved timidly and decided that he might quiet the crowd and tamp down the enthusiasm by walking around the court and engaging as many people as possible. As he made the circuit, the crowd noise did abate somewhat as individuals called out to him, replacing the coordinated cheering and chants. He was grateful that his crowd control plan seemed to be working.

As he approached mid court, opposite where he had entered, he stopped suddenly. His heart seemed to skip a beat when he saw the guidon and the man waving it. There with a big grin was the unmistakable figure of First Sergeant Cole. His military style haircut and stocky body adorned with a jungle fatigue jacket left no doubt that here was a friend of Marco's from his army days.

Again, Tony's first thought was how Marco would react when he saw this key person from his suppressed past. For the first time, Tony had some real doubts about his own efforts in staging such a public spectacle. His heart sank as he thought about the overload that this event could have on Marco's fragile psyche.

He gave a timid wave in response to Sergeant Cole's enthusiastic waving of the guidon. He took a deep breath. At that moment, it became clear to Tony that Marco's hour of reckoning was upon him whether he was ready or not. Tony knew that the way things were unfolding could either get Marco to snap out of his psychological problem or push him further into depression. Things were happening so quickly, Tony felt he had lost control of the situation. He had spent much of the time since Vietnam managing Marco's environment, trying to lead him slowly out of the darkness. He was afraid that this night might be too big a leap for Marco to make.

Tony had a long moment of remorse thinking about his involvement in setting up this match. He thought back to all the things he had done over the last few weeks to bring his friend against his will, to this emotionally charged evening. Now it was here and there was no turning back, for better or for worse.

He smiled, took a deep breath and began the climb into the bleachers to greet Sergeant Cole.

"Tony, Tony wait for me." He recognized the voice and turn to see Justine running toward him. He embraced her tightly and said," Boy, am I glad to see you. I really need you tonight."

"I'm so happy to hear that because I need you and I need to be part of this. I never realized how much I missed you and the memories we shared until I saw you in Dallas. I knew then that I had boarded up the wrong window. Once I removed the barriers I found the light and warmth I had lost," Justine said looking up at him.

Tony kissed her gently on the lips." I'm not sure I understand all of that, but I'm grateful for whatever remodeling you did that brought you here. I wasn't so sure a moment ago, but now I think this is going to be a great evening. He took her hand and led her into the bleachers.

"Well, Top I didn't expect to see you here," He said as he reached Sergeant Cole." How did you find out about the place and time of the match?"

"Captain Saunders here notified us all. I wouldn't have missed this for anything," he answered stepping aside to reveal Chuck behind him.

Chuck leaned forward from his position which has been obscured by the sergeant. He gave a weak smile and a timid wave to Tony and said sheepishly," Hi Tony fancy meeting you here."

Before Tony could react, Terry, Bob and Tommy stood up in the row beyond Chuck."Wow, this is really some coincidence. All of us decided to attend the same tennis match. What are the chances of that?" Bob said with a loud guffaw.

"I should have known that Chuck would be the organizer of this spontaneous reunion," Tony said as he moved down the row to greet each of them.

"Yup," They all said in unison.

"And you Justine? How did you get here?" Tony turned back to her.

Justine gave a nod toward Chuck and said," That would be a yup for me too," she said with a grin.

"You know I've always said there are three means of communication, telephone, telegraph and tell Chuck. In any event I'm happy to see you all, I think." Tony said as he shook each man's hand again.

"Let's go behind the bleachers and have a battalion meeting," Chuck said as he pushed Tony back out into the aisle.

As Tony started down the bleacher steps the crowd again erupted into a cheer,"Ton-ee, Ton-ee." Tony waved weakly to the fans and made his way quickly out of the stands followed by Justine and his friends.

"And I thought foolishly that this was Marco's night," Bob said with a loud laugh as they reached an un-congested area behind the bleachers. "But then again, no one remembers the name of the guy who was shot out of the cannon. However, everyone knows who PT Barnum was," Chuck said as he slapped Tony on the back.

They all laughed as they gathered in a tight circle." Okay, time to get down to business," Chuck said seriously." Listen Tony we all talked it over and we think it's time for an intervention with Marco. The First Sergeant here has taken the lead on this effort, so I'd like him to explain it. Top, it's all yours," he said as he turned to Sergeant Cole.

"Sir," he said as he positioned himself in front of Tony." I don't mean to be disrespectful, but you have tried your gentle officer approach with Captain Covello for twenty years now without much success. I believe it's time for a little drill sergeant tough love. Your way obviously hasn't worked, so it's time for a new approach. That's why we're all here. We all agree that there should be no more tiptoe-ing around starting tonight. I don't believe we should be trying to prevent the old man from confronting his past any longer." Sergeant Cole put his hands on his hips while he awaited Tony's reply.

Tony looked into the faces of his friends around him. He stared an extra moment at Justine's striking blue eyes. He had forgotten how beautiful and compassionate those eyes were. For a second, he recalled seeing those eyes in his darkest moments when he lay gravely wounded in the hospital at Pleiku. He remembered that it was those eyes that had drawn him back from the edge of the abyss and back to the world of the living. He finally said," You too Justine? You believe Marco needs tough love right now?"

"Yes, Tony I believe that's what he needs," she said softly.

He turned at last to Terry who stood slightly behind Chuck. Tony moved closer to him so he could see him more clearly." And what about you Terry? You were pretty adamant about not getting involved in any of this when we saw you in your mountain hideout."

Terry looked down at the ground. When he raised his eyes, he looked at his friends and then at Tony." Your visit to my cabin started me thinking about the whole Vietnam thing. In my efforts to forget about that crummy year I was forgetting about you guys and the great bonds and friendships we developed that year. In effect, I was doing what the country did-forgetting the war and all those who fought in it. I didn't want to do that any longer." He paused for a moment, then said firmly," I believe now it's time for all of us to come home together."

They were all silent for a moment, then spontaneously embraced."Okay. Here's what I'm going to do," Tony said as he stepped back. "I'm going back into that locker room and I'm going to tell Marco that you're here along with several hundred other people. I'm not going to mention you just yet Top because too much at one time could spook him. And, I'm going to tell him he has to suck it up and soundly defeat the great white whale for everyone who came out to support him. That's it, no ifs, ands or buts."

"Thata boy Tony. I'm feeling good that that's exactly what is needed right now," Bob said in support.

"I like the plan sir, with one minor change. I believe Lieutenant Ryan should go in there with you for backup," Sergeant Cole said.

Tony looked at the sergeant for a moment and said,"I believe you're right Top. Marco's a tough nut. It won't hurt to have him out-numbered." He shook hands with them all and gave Justine a quick kiss." Come on Terry," he said as he started to leave."It's time to get our boy ready." He turned back to the group."By the way, the name of the guy who was shot out of Barnum's cannon was Umberto the Magnificent."

They all stared at him silently for a moment before pushing him away." Save that BS for Marco," Chuck yelled after them as Tony and Terry hurried toward the locker room.

* * * *

"Tony where have you been?" Marco asked as he got up from the bench. "It sounds like the whole town is out there. What's going on?"

"Well, yes it does seem like there's a bigger turnout than we expected. But, that doesn't change anything. Actually, it's better this way. There'll be more witnesses to your decisive crushing of El Waspo Grande."

"Oh my God…" Marco groaned.

"Hey, look who's here," Tony turned aside and brought Terry forward." It's the recon platoon leader. Remember how we both thought we wouldn't see much of him after our visit to his hideout in the mountains. Well, here he is to lend you his support."

Terry stepped forward and gave Marco a big hug." We're all so proud of you Marco. I know that you wouldn't have chosen to do things this way. But, now that it's here, I know you'll give it your best like you did with every other mission you were given."

Marco held onto his friend's arms for a moment." How did the Pied Piper get you involved in this? I thought you wanted to bury anything that reminded you of Vietnam."

"Actually, Tony had nothing to do with it. Chuck called me and told me about the match. I've been doing a lot of thinking since you guys visited me at my cabin. I just decided I wanted to come out of the darkness. I figured out that I was letting that year in Vietnam poison the rest of my life. I vowed not to let that happen anymore." Terry stared into his friend's eyes for a moment." It's time for you to let it go too Marco," he said softly.

Marco let go of Terry's arms and stepped back."Maybe you're right Terry. I'm tired. I'm tired of trying to manage my memories so that I never think about Vietnam. I'm tired of watching everyone tiptoe around me because they're afraid I'm going to explode. I am tired of tiptoeing around myself because I'm afraid of what will happen if I let myself think about Vietnam or more specifically that awful day. I've been doing some thinking myself since I reconnected with everyone on the trip. I already let Vietnam ruin a bunch of years. I'm not going to let it ruin any more." He and Terry embraced again.

"Whaaaaat?" Tony yelled." Who are you and what did you do with my friend Marco? I've been trying to get him to say those words for 20 years."

"Asshole," Marco said with a grin." Let's get this dumb match started so I can get my boring life back."

"Good idea pal let's finish this up whoever you are before Marco gets back," Tony said as he slapped his friend on the back. The three of them linked arms and marched resolutely to the door leading to the tennis court.

Tony stepped out first. There was a murmur and then a harsh silence when the crowd saw him. When Marco moved toward the court the audience erupted in a loud cheer," Mar-co, Mar-co."

When he heard it, Marco stopped and subconsciously took a step backward. Terry grabbed his arm and gently nudged him towards the court. The cheering got louder when the rest of the crowd saw them making their way to the player's bench.

"Okay Marco. There's the target out there. That big white whale," Tony said pointing to Barrington on the bench opposite them. He was dressed in a stylish black and white warm-up suit. His black tennis shoes matched the outfit exactly. Marco was sorry now that he hadn't purchased a new warm-up suit for the match.

Barrington moved confidently on to the court, motioning Marco to do the same. A chorus of boos and cat calls greeted him as he took his place at one end of the court. His smile, almost a smirk showed he was enjoying the attention, even if it was negative.

Tony positioned himself directly in front of Marco."Okay pal. Remember, nothing fancy. Just keep the ball in play and make the whale move around as much as possible. He looks like he's huffing and puffing already."

Marco tried to see around Tony so he could scan the crowd. Tony saw him and said firmly," Pal, concentrate. The only person that matters in this building is Howell. Focus," Tony commanded.

"I just wanted to see which of the other guys are here," Marco said as he stood."Who else is here?"

"Just Chuck and a few of the others. That shouldn't make any difference to you. Get out there and make us proud. Remember, run his ass off even during the warm-up," Tony slapped him on the back.

As Marco ran onto the court the crowd again erupted it into a loud cheer. He gave a feeble wave of his racquet as he took his position in the far end of the court.

Barrington acknowledged Marco with a big smile and a crisp salute with his racquet. The two men started to hit soft shots back and forth. After a few moments, Howell quickened the pace by hitting some sharp shots past Marco. With each passed shot the crowd moaned, then cheered with each shot he returned. Barrington moved gracefully around the court, easily running down Marco's returns. Marco continued to scan the crowd between shots, clearly disrupting the flow of his movements. After some practice serves both men returned to their benches for a short rest.

"Marco what are you doing out there? You look like you're totally distracted. You better wake up and focus or tonight is going to be an embarrassment for all of us." Tony was obviously irritated by his friend's early performance and disappointed by the sudden reversal of Marco's mood.

"You went too far this time Tony. You shouldn't have invited all of our friends. Who else did you invite? Tell me now, so I won't have to keep looking into the stands to find out myself," Marco glared at his friend.

Tony was equally angry."First off pal, I didn't invite anyone. Chuck did. I wouldn't have done it because I know how you are. I've spent over twenty years trying to protect you from yourself. I'm tired of doing it and I'm not going to do it any longer," he had to yell to overcome the crowd noise.

Terry stepped between them." What's the matter with you guys? You have several hundred people who have come out to support both of you and you're fighting like you're in your own living room. Now suck it up and give these people what they came for. At least give them an honest effort."

Tony straightened up and smiled as he patted Marco on the shoulder." I'm sorry Marco. Once again, it's the recon platoon leader who injects some calm wisdom into our petty brawl. Let's humiliate that big tub of crap first and then we can finish the fight later. Is it a deal?" Tony stuck his hand out.

Marco looked up at Tony for a moment then took his hand."It's a deal."

"How is he doing Tony?" The familiar voice startled Tony. He turned and saw the smiling face of Rudy Baer who greeted him and Marco.

"He'll do a lot better now that you're here, that's for sure. He sure needs your help" Tony said as he nudged Rudy a short distance away from Marco."He's totally distracted. I don't think he's using any of the things you taught him. I can tell he's right on the edge of one of his retreats into the past. My friends and I were trying to use this match as a sort of intervention. I'm not sure now that was such a good idea. But we're here now, so we have to make it work. Your arrival was a godsend. If you'll do it, I believe it would be better if you coach him while I momentarily fade away."

"Well, I'm willing to do it if Marco's okay with it. Let's ask him," Rudy said as they both moved back to Marco's side.

"I'm good," Marco said after they explained the plan.

Just then, the umpire motioned Marco and Barrington to join him at his chair in the center of the court. Rudy accompanied Marco while Henry followed Howell to the short meeting.

Barrington, smiling broadly extended his hand to Marco and then to Rudy." Well your big night has finally arrived Covello. I see you and your buddy DeJulio had to turn this into a dago festival instead of allowing it to be a tennis match with some decorum," he said looking at Marco. "However, this spectacle is fine with me. Humiliating you in front of so many people ought to keep you and your friend DeJulio quiet for a long time."

Marco appeared not to hear Howell. He was continuing to search the bleachers.

"It's obvious from your remarks that you're interested in establishing a level of decorum right from the outset," Rudy said sarcastically.

"Who are you?" Barrington asked sharply shifting his gaze to Rudy.

"Just a friend interested in seeing that the best man wins," Rudy said with a big smile.

"Gentlemen may I have your attention please," the umpire said.

Rudy pulled Marco closer to him and said, "Marco pay attention here."

Marco looked away from his search of the audience and said," Oh yeah. Sorry Rudy."

"We'll play the best of three sets. As soon as one of you wins two sets, the match is over. Since we have no line judges, I will make all calls as to what is in or out. All of my decisions are final. There is no appeal. Is that clear?" The umpire instructed.

"That's okay with me," Barrington said as he shook the umpire's hand.

"It's okay with us," Rudy said. He liked the decisiveness of the umpire. He grabbed Marco's arm and nudged him back to the bench."Marco I don't know what's wrong with you and I don't care. But I went out of my way to get you ready for tonight. Whether you like it or not a lot of people have brought their support and reputations here including me. We're all counting on you to at least try your hardest and do your best whether you win or not. Tonight is much bigger than you and whatever emotional hang up you're dealing with. Is that clear?" Rudy said sharply.

"Y.eah, it's clear Rudy. I'm sorry", Marco paused for a moment and looked beyond Rudy.

"I'm sorry. I thought I was emotionally ready to deal with tonight. However, there is someone here that knocked down all of the walls I've built to insulate myself from some memories I wanted to avoid. I wish he hadn't come."

"Well, he did come. And there are about 500 people, including me who don't give a rat's ass about what walls got knocked down and who knocked them down. They care only about you putting forth your best effort to take down a big blowhard." Rudy paused for a moment."Marco, I know we can do this together. Lets get it done."

Marco took a deep breath. He looked steadily at Rudy for a minute." Okay coach, let's do it," he said finally. He then ran back on to the court, occasionally still scanning the bleachers. Once he settled into position, Barrington served. It was a blistering serve that blasted by Marco. It took several more serves before Marco got in sync with the speed of his opponent's serve. The score was 40– love before Marco managed a feeble return that Barrington then drilled past him to end the first game. A low, audible moan rose from the crowd each time that Barrington powered the ball past Marco.

By the third game, Marco was coping better with the speed of Barrington's play. He was returning the balls more consistently. None of his returns were winners, but he was keeping the ball in play. That was the strategy that Rudy had drilled into him. He wanted Marco to be the backboard, returning as many balls as he could to Barrington. If he could make Barrington move to either side or front to back, that would be even better.

It wasn't until game four that Marco won his first game. The crowd, finally with something to cheer, let out a huge roar. During that game, there were subtle hints that Rudy picked up confirming that his strategy of moving Barrington around was the correct one. It was obvious that Howell had done nothing to condition himself for the match. Clearly, he had come to the match expecting his substantial tennis skills to prevail without much effort.

As Marco sat down next to Rudy during the break, he once again scanned the crowd. Rudy stood in front of him trying to block his view while he tried to coach Marco. His gaze became fixed as he seemed to find what he was looking for. His eyes narrowed and then widened, a look of fear clearly showing on his entire face.

Rudy was so struck by Marco's reaction, that he turned to look at whatever had transfixed him. He immediately saw a stocky man yelling and waving a guidon vigorously. When Rudy turned to face him, he saw that Marco now sat limply on the bench, his head lowered and his eyes on the ground.

"I… I can't go back out there Rudy," Marcos said in a hoarse voice.

"Oh yes you can Marco, and yes you will," Rudy said forcefully."I am way out on a limb with this whole project. When word gets out that I and my training center were the major resource you used, my reputation will be all intertwined in what you do here tonight. I went out of my way to help you and I'll be damned if I'm going to let you punish me for my generosity. Now get out there," Rudy said angrily.

Marco looked at him for a moment, then moved slowly back onto the court. As he shuffled back to his position, he kept glancing at the section of the audience where he had seen Sergeant Cole.

The remaining two games were a disaster for Marco. He lost the first game without getting a point. He managed only one point in the second game.

Barrington, the winner of the first set, 6-1, waved his racquet triumphantly and used it to applaud himself, taunting the crowd. His actions elicited a strong chorus of boos from the audience. While everyone was focused on Barrington's antics in the center of the court, hardly anyone noticed that Marco left the court and moved quickly to the locker room. He was followed closely by Rudy and Tony.

When they found him, he was sitting on a bench, his head hanging almost to his knees. He still held the racquet in his trembling right hand. He didn't look up when they approached him.

"What do you think you're doing Marco?" Tony yelled at him." You at least owe it to those people out there to finish the match."

Marco didn't look up. The trembling of his arm seemed to get worse.

Rudy stared silently at the broken figure of his student for a moment before he turned to Tony."I'm not sure of what's going on here, but I believe this match is over. He's in no condition to continue playing. In fairness to everyone out there, we should go out and concede the match," there was sadness but also resignation in Rudy's voice.

Tony walked over and put his hand on Marco shoulder. His friend never moved. He kept his eyes on the ground, the racquet shaking in his clenched right hand. Tony faced Rudy and said softly,"I believe you're right. I was always afraid there was an outside chance that all of this would prove to be too much for Marco. However, I really thought he was strong enough coming into tonight. These last few days he appeared to be more squared away then I've seen him in some time. It seemed that the support of his girlfriend Kathy and some of his Vietnam buddies helped him to come out of the darkness. It's clear now that I was wrong." Tony looked back at Marco." I was wrong," he said sadly.

"What the hell is going on in here?" Sergeant Cole's loud voice overwhelmed the muted discussion between Tony and Rudy." Where the hell are you?" he yelled impatiently.

"Back here, Top," Tony answered.

Sgt. Cole came striding purposefully into the row of lockers where Marco was sitting. He held the guidon horizontally in his right hand so that it pointed like a spear at Rudy and Tony." What happened out there?" He asked as he approached the men." That soft, fat whale was beginning to tire when you let up on him. I can tell an undisciplined, out of shape loser a mile away. That guy is the poster boy of losers. Why didn't you keep his ass running out there sir?" He looked down at Marco as if noticing him for the first time.

Marco slowly raised his head and looked up at him. His eyes widened and his face contorted as if he were seeing some grotesque image. Their eyes locked for a moment before Marco lowered his head again.

Sergeant Cole stared at him for a moment before turning to Rudy and Tony as if seeking an explanation. Tony met his gaze and said softly," I'm sorry Top, the game is over. There's nothing more to do. We're getting ready to go out there and concede the match."

Sergeant Cole stared at Tony for a moment, then looked back at Marco's trembling and defeated figure. He looked at the sorry image of his broken former company commander. Everyone was silent before he raised the guidon and slammed it into the concrete floor and yelled," No." The sound of the staff hitting the floor with such force reverberated through the empty locker room like a shot. Marco recoiled involuntarily. He shot a quick look at his former First Sergeant before he lowered his head again.

"I can't believe you're going to concede to that tub of blubber out there. Why he couldn't make his way through even one repetition of the daily dozen. And that's who you're surrendering to?" Sergeant Cole moved closer to Marco to emphasize his disgust at what was happening." I talked to some of the boys in the company who said they would try to be here. I'm glad now that they didn't come. I'd hate for them to see you like this, a totally beaten shell of the man they all admired so much. To a man, they all thought you were the best officer they served with. It's better that they retain the image of you in Vietnam as a hard charging, never-say-die leader instead of this pathetic picture of you feeling sorry for yourself." Sergeant Cole paused and looked down at Marco. He didn't move as the words rained down on him.

"Those young men trusted you and would have followed you anywhere. Under your leadership the company did a lot of good things under some very difficult conditions. Yes, it was a crummy war, but we did the best we could, and that effort was pretty damn good." Sergeant Cole crouched down to get closer to Marco's face.

"And you, you were the glue that held it altogether through some pretty tough times," he said thrusting his finger at Marco's bowed head." If you choose to focus only on the few bad things that happened and ignore all that we accomplished, then I feel sorry for you." He stood up and stared down at Marco. He lowered his voice and said,"You know what really ticks me off? What really ticks me off is that by you skulking around you're confirming for those that opposed us that what we did was wrong and we should somehow be ashamed."

He stepped back from Marco and leaned on the guidon which he still held in his right hand. He seemed to be exhausted by the effort to move Marco.

"It's okay Top. I believe we all did everything we could," Tony said as he put his arm around the sergeant's. shoulder. "You better go out there and concede the match now Rudy."

Without saying a word, Rudy left and returned to the court.

"Let me have that club or bat or whatever you call it. I'm going to use it to beat the crap out of that arrogant opponent of yours," Sergeant Cole said as he viciously ripped the racquet from Marco's trembling hand. He turned to leave and then turned back to Marco. "Here's what I do know for sure. We let them steal our honor during and after the war. We can't let them continue to do it. At least I'm not going to let them continue to do it." He turned on his heels and left the locker room.

After a moment, Tony followed him without looking back at Marco.

Tony and Sergeant Cole joined Rudy at the umpire's chair. A Smiling Barrington and Henry were also there. From time to time, Howell raised his racquet or gave the two finger victory sign to the buzzing crowd. Each gesture was met by boos which only inspired Barrington to repeat them.

Sergeant Cole, still holding the guidon in one hand and the tennis racquet in the other inched closer to Howell. The sergeant began bumping into him, softly at first then more violently as Howell continued his taunting of the crowd."What the hell are you doing?" He said as he tried to get away from the pushing.

Tony grabbed Sergeant Cole by the arm and pulled him away from Howell. Sergeant Cole glared at Barrington as Tony put himself between the two men.

"What's going on? Where's Covello?" The umpire asked.

"He's um – not coming out. He's decided to withdraw from the match," Rudy said hesitatingly.

"Oh, too bad," Howell's grin widened."It's too bad he decided to throw in the towel so quickly. I would have enjoyed beating him decisively in front of this crowd so that I don't have to endure any more of your or his smart ass comments," Barrington said looking directly at Tony.

Sergeant Cole tried to get around Tony and get to Barrington, but was restrained by him." Top, please let's not make this worse than it already is. I know how you feel. I feel the exact same way. But, we lost and we need to be as dignified as we can be in front of all these people."

"Okay, but I need to make some sort of announcement to the audience. What do you want me to say?" The umpire looked at both Rudy and Barrington.

"Well, I don't want to embarrass DeJulio's little friend any more than necessary. Let's just say he twisted his ankle and can't continue," Barrington said with a wink at Tony.

"And why don't I say it was an involuntary twitch I had right after I punch you in the mouth," Sergeant Cole said with a wink at Barrington as he tried to move past Tony again.

Howell took an involuntary step backward before Tony could grab the sergeant's arm and pull him back. He glared at Barrington for a moment before Tony was able to get between the two men again.

"Okay, I'll make the announcement... the umpires voice was drowned out by a huge cheer from the audience. The men at the center of the court stared at one another and then at the crowd to determine the cause of the uproar. They followed where the crowd was looking and pointing. It was only then that they saw Marco emerging from the locker room and striding purposefully to the bench at mid court.

Tony and Sergeant Cole left immediately to join Marco. Rudy stayed with the umpire and Howell.

"Let me have that bat or club or whatever you call it you old, tired broken down excuse for a First Sergeant," Marco said with a smirk when they joined him.

Sergeant Cole stared at him as if he were seeing a ghost. He didn't move even after Marco yanked the racquet from his hand. He looked into his old company commander's eyes for a moment before he jumped up with a resounding yell," Uh-rah." He began to waive the guidon violently in the direction of his friends in the bleachers. Soon there was a steady chant of 'Uh-rah' from that section of the stands that was quickly picked up by the entire audience. The noise of the continuous cheer and the stamping of feet made it impossible to communicate in the gym.

Tony got close to Marco and yelled in his ear, "Are you ready?"

Marco pinched Tony's cheek and said,"Let's go Mr. Barnum," barely audible over the crowd noise.

Tony gave his friend a hug and turned back to the umpire's chair where Rudy and Howell still waited. He gave a thumbs up with a huge smile.

Barrington, somewhat unnerved by the crowd pandemonium and the change of events, smiled grimly. The umpire issued final instructions to Howell and Rudy before they moved back to their respective benches and prepared to resume the match.

"Remember Marco, no fancy stuff. Just try to be a human backboard out there. I've seen his type many times before. He's a blowhard surrounded by too many pounds of blubber. If you can keep him running his body and inflated ego will both explode. Just keep the ball in play. Is that clear?" Rudy yelled in Marco's face as the crowd mayhem continued unabated around them.

"It's clear coach," Marco yelled back.

As Marco took his place on the court, the crowd noise became even louder. It was only when Barrington fired a serve past him for an ace that the noise level was reduced somewhat. It rose again, however when Howell got ready for his second serve.

Marco managed a weak return which Barrington charged and quickly converted into a passing shot that Marco was unable to get. Marco lost the first three games. However, the velocity and sharpness of Barrington's serves and shots slowed perceptively by the end of the third game. He stood with his hands on his hips in between serves. His breathing became heavier, unnoticeable at first, then clearly visible.

Marco was able to hit a gentle lob to win the fourth game when Barrington was unable to run it down. Perspiration ran down his face and his elegant tennis shirt and shorts were darkened and sweat stained.

Howell won the next game when Marco's lob was too long. Barrington barely tried to get to the ball, but was saved because the shot was too long. With Howell ahead four games to one in the second set, it looked grim for Marco. However, it was also clear at that point that Howell was physically worn down. He lingered a few extra minutes at each break. He was also consuming copious amounts of water. It was clear that the tide was slowly turning in Marco's favor. The question was simply one of determining if Barrington could end the match quickly before his physical tank hit empty.

In game six, Marco sensing that the momentum had shifted, began to rush the net, easily putting away Howells increasingly weak shots from the baseline. Barrington made fewer and fewer attempts to leave the deepest part of the court, hoping instead to drive some shots down the alley past Marco. However, Marco was everywhere. He seemed to gain strength and energy as the match progressed. The second set ended when Marco won the tiebreaker, eleven to nine.

At the beginning of the third set, the crowd sensed that Barrington was finished. In between serves, he tried to catch his breath by bending over at the waist and taking huge breaths. He also began to dispute all close line calls even though he was not near many of them.

The crowd began to chant 'Goodbye Howell', followed by 'Uh-rah' when Marco went up three games to love in the third set. By the time the set ended at six to zero, Howell was not even making an attempt to chase down anything not hit right at him.

The crowd surged on to the court after the end of the match and raised Marco on their shoulders and marched him around the facility. Barrington sat on his bench with his head hung down almost between his knees, obviously exhausted. To Tony it seemed like an ironic and pathetic replay of Marco's posture of several hours earlier. He knew, that Barrington's momentary defeat was just that– momentary. He knew that by Monday, Howell would reclaim his arrogance and disdain for all people and things that didn't meet his standards. Whereas Marco had just now emerged from a tortuous over twenty years of self-doubt. With the rise of one man and the fall of another tonight, perhaps the universe was a tiny bit more in balance he thought.

CHAPTER TWENTY

THE BACHELOR PARTY

"What a great idea Tony," Chuck said as he leaned back against the stones of the fireplace. They all sat on the floor or on makeshift stools in the cabin." Having Marco's bachelor party in Terry's cabin is a stroke of genius."

"Yeah, anybody can arrange a bachelor party in a swank and luxurious hotel like the Ritz or Marriott. It takes a real, how should I say this, a real master of uncouth understatement to plan a party in a primitive setting in a forest like this location," Bob added.

"Ah– yes. Criticism from two connoisseurs of the highlife, who spent the better part of a year eating out of cans. All while sampling the culture and sophistication experienced only by those bon vivants privileged enough to travel along the remote Cambodian border during wartime. Your credentials certainly qualify you to critique my choice of venue for accommodations and dining," Tony responded.

"Before this gets too far out of hand, I'd like to point out that you bozos voluntarily and readily traveled from near and far to get here as soon as you received Tony's invitation," Marco added with a smile.

"Touché," Chuck said as he stood up." No matter how bizarre the scheme, it does seem like we always respond to the Pied Piper's call. I propose a toast to Tony, the Pied Piper."

They all stood, raised their beers and shouted,"To the Pied Piper." After a swig of beer, they all set down again.

"And I would like to propose a toast to the prospective bridegroom who is the recipient of more good fortune than he deserves. This slayer of the WASP King, the winner of the hand of the fair Kathy and the gent who will soon willingly and eagerly leave the ranks of bachelorhood, I give you Marco the Magnificent," Tony raised his beer.

They all jumped to their feet again, hoisting their beers and shouting, "To the groom, to Marco."

After gathering around Marco and slapping him on the back, they resumed sitting once again. Tony waited until they were completely settled before he proposed another toast." I would also like to propose a toast"… he was interrupted by a chorus of groans and boos from his friends.

"Tony, this up-and-down business is like doing the daily dozen. Could you please do all the toasts while we're standing," Chuck pleaded.

"I would also like to propose a toast," Tony continued ignoring the cat calls from his friends." I propose a toast to our other honored guest. She's a combat hardened veteran, the pride of the Pleiku MASH who has the undying gratitude from a multitude of wounded grunts, especially yours truly. I give you the loveliest and most talented honorary member of the First Battalion, 14th infantry, First Lieutenant Justine O'Reilly."

They all jumped to their feet loudly cheering, then ran to Justine and hugged her. When they returned to their positions around the room, she held up her hand. The room became totally silent.

"You'll never know how honored I am to share not only this wonderful evening with you all, but how touched I am to be included in what I know is a very close brotherhood. Although I wasn't on the battlefield with you, in a very small way I feel I shared the hardships of combat with you by looking into the eyes of your wounded comrades and hearing their anguished cries at night." She looked around the room at each of them before she said," I'd like to propose my own toast. To the bonds and friendship we all share, forged in adversity and tempered by the memories we all cherish." She raised her beer to the exuberant shouts echoing off the walls of the small cabin.

"Here, here."

Beau, Terry's golden retriever, who had been resting near the fireplace, moved to the door with an annoyed look at the raucous group.

Tony moved quickly to Justine's side and gave her a kiss on the cheek." Is she great or what?" He said as he held her tightly around her waist.

"Okay, Tony. Before I sit down one last time, are you going to make any more toasts?" Chuck asked.

"Why yes, my perceptive friend. I do have one more announcement and a toast," he said as he pulled Justine closer to him." Justine and I are getting married."

The crowd erupted in a huge cheer and rushed to the couple, congratulating them.

After a moment, Tony held up his hand to quiet the group. When they were silent he said," I don't know how or why I let her get away from me in 1967, but I guarantee she won't get away from me this time."

Tony's declaration was met with a raucous response as the group crowded in closer to him and Justine to renew their congratulations.

Chuck held up his hand for silence." Tony what finally convinced you to pop the question? Was it because Justine saved your life or because she can throw a hand grenade further than you can?"

"Both," Tony yelled over the noise of his friends' celebration of his announcement.

"I'm done. It's time to begin the sampling of the culinary delights befitting such a renowned group of gourmands here assembled," He said as he and Justine moved to a pile of boxes stacked near the door. He reached into one of the containers and withdrew an olive drab can." First and foremost of course, is everyone's favorite, ham and lima beans." He threw the can to Chuck while the group booed and hissed." Followed closely by turkey loaf," he said as he tossed another can to Marco as the booing became louder. "Well then, how about pound cake and fruit cocktail," he said to the cheers of the group.

While Tony taunted his friends, Justine spread a paper tablecloth on the sole table in the cabin. She unpacked napkins, utensils and candles which she lit and placed on several surfaces around the big open room. She then unpacked a large quantity of pizzas and sub sandwiches which she stacked on the table.

When the men saw what Justine was doing, they rushed over to her and selected items from the table while Tony continued pulling packages and cans from the box in front of him. "How about cheese and crackers," he yelled even though no one was paying attention to him." I can see you uncouth bozos have no appreciation for the nostalgia that food can evoke," he said to no one in particular as he moved to the table Justine had set.

The noise was replaced by conversations throughout the cabin where the men settled down to eat and drink. Soon there was a contented buzz in the room.

As the men finished eating, Justine stood up. The room became silent."Before you guys drift off, I think we should all remember why we're here. It's to honor the groom to be– Marco."

Loud cheers again erupted from the crowd. Justine held up her hand to quiet the group once more." Gentlemen, I give you the soon to be husband of sweet Kathy-Marco Covello."

Another loud cheer and the stamping of feet shook the cabin. Beau, from his position near the door, raised his head and gave another annoyed look at the men.

Marco stood and waited for the crowd to settle down. When they were quiet, he said with a smile," Unaccustomed as I am to public speaking..." he was interrupted by a loud chorus of boos and cat calls.

He held up his hand so he could continue." Unlike my silver tongued friend, Tony, I'm not such a good speaker. However, I'm happy to have this opportunity to tell you about several important things. First, how Kathy and I got together and how she and Tony have helped me come out of the darkness I was in after Vietnam. Secondly, I would like to relate a story about a trip that Sergeant Cole and I took that was extremely important to my ultimate rehabilitation.

"The great thing about Kathy and me is that our relationship developed right under your noses. While you guys were yukking it up and cavorting with all of those Texas beauties, Kathy and I were exchanging phone calls. Our first date was a classic Italian rendezvous-in an Italian bakery. I told her about the great pastries at Angelo's and that I went there every Saturday morning to pick up baked goods for my parents. She showed up at Angelo's soon after I told her that. We started that morning with a coffee and a cannoli. Our secret meetings soon included lunches and then frequent dinners. We were careful to make sure that no one learned of our growing relationship.

"That is until the town busybody- Tony," at the mention of Tony's name the crowd booed, "and Kathy's friend, the town yenta–Debbie," the crowd booed again even though they didn't know Debbie-"found us at Mario's restaurant one night. They had suspected that something was up, so they got together and compared notes. It wasn't long after that that they tracked us down.

"We finally confessed over manicotti and meatballs that we had been seeing one another and that we were in love. It's well known in Italian circles that manicotti and meatballs have some secret ingredient that makes people unable to lie and causes them to confess."

A loud chorus of laughter, boos and cat calls greeted Marco's telling of the story. He held up his hand again. When the crowd quieted down he continued." It's true, Mussolini used to torture people by serving them manicotti and meatballs to extract valuable information from his enemies."

Wadded up napkins and plastic utensils pelted Marco as he made this last pronouncement.

After the rain of objects ceased he continued,"Judging by that immature outburst, I'm guessing you all are questioning my knowledge of Italian folklore." He smiled and paused for a minute, looking at his friends seated around the room. When he continued, his smile had vanished and his voice took on a more somber tone." Well, here's something you can believe." He paused again and pulled up a chair. He sat down and looked at his clenched hands for a moment before he spoke."If it weren't for Kathy and my friend Tony pushing and prodding me to confront my demons, I don't know what would've happened to me. And this is where the second part of my story comes in– my trip with Sergeant Cole. He looked down at his hands again before he shifted his gaze to the sergeant who was sitting quietly in the corner of the cabin.

"Kathy and Tony convinced me to seek counseling at the VA. I finally did that. With their help and my especially my counselor's help, I was able finally to talk about some events and issues I had suppressed for many years. Because of their support, I made rapid progress. However, there was one memory, one event, I couldn't deal with no matter how hard I tried. It was when my RTO was killed." Marco's voice trailed off to almost a whisper. He paused looking down again at his tightly clenched hands.

When he looked up there were tears in his eyes. The room was totally silent. The only noise in the cabin was the sound of the shutters being beaten gently against the windows by the wind." I... I just couldn't get over the guilt I felt over that's fine young soldier's death. More importantly, I couldn't get over the sorrow and anguish I felt I had caused his family. That's why I was filled with so much fear and dread when I received Sergeant Cole's phone call and proposal. I later found out that Kathy, Tony and the sergeant were all in on the plan. However, when I first spoke to Sergeant Cole I didn't know that.

"In any event, he called me and suggested that we visit Specialist Golinski's family. At first, I adamantly refused. I made all kinds of excuses. When they wouldn't accept my excuses I tried to postpone the visit saying that my recovery was still too fragile for such an emotional meeting. In the end, the three of them prevailed and I very reluctantly agreed to visit Golinski's family.

* * * *

Marco anxiously scanned the crowd at the gate looking for Sergeant Cole. Except for a few early glitches, the flight into Detroit had been uneventful. In spite of that, all of his fears and uncertainty about the trip had returned with a vengeance. He decided that if his old Field First hadn't been able to make the trip for some reason, he would abort the visit and return home on the next available flight.

As his apprehension rose he finally saw the sergeant standing away from the crowd, legs apart and hands on his hips. He looked like he was disgusted by the lack of discipline of the crowd and was about ready to order them into a military formation. Marco smiled in relief at seeing him. He felt some of his fears subside as he glimpsed the resolute confidence and bearing of the old soldier.

"Good to see you again sir," Sergeant Cole said as he reached for Marco's hand and clasped him on the arm.

Marco looked at his old friend and noticed immediately the blue eyes which blazed with an intensity that Marco remembered from the many assignments they had shared 25 years earlier."It's good to see you again Sergeant Cole. I'm so glad you're here. It looks like we get to share one more mission. And, just like in the old days I'll be leaning on you to make it a successful one."

"Yup, sir. Just like the old days. And like all the others, we'll make this one successful also," Sergeant Cole said with a smile.

Marco felt his confidence returning as they made their way out of the concourse and into the terminal. Neither man spoke as they strode quickly to the exit. Once outside, the harsh January wind took away their breath momentarily.

Inside the cab, Marco took a deep breath, calming himself from the rapid sequence of events which had brought him to Detroit. He had left New Jersey at 6 AM this morning. Tony and Kathy had both gone with him to the airport, leaving their homes at 4:30. After brief goodbyes, Marco had boarded the flight. Although the plane taxied quickly out to the runway, the flight had been delayed by a faulty indicator light. Marco was conflicted by the delay. On the one hand, now that he was committed he wanted to complete the visit. On the other hand, postponement would give him more time to prepare for the encounter with the young soldier's family.

However, after 30 minutes the decision was out of Marco's hands again when the pilot announced that the problem was fixed. As the plane rolled down the runway, his dread and anxiety returned with more intensity. Now in the cab with Sgt. Cole he began again to focus on the visit."Tell me again how this all came about"

"You remember our company clerk Specialist Emory. Well, he called me a few months ago."

"Of course I remember Emory. He was a good soldier and a very smart young man. When he came into the company, I knew right away that we desperately needed him to bring some order and organization to the orderly room. He wanted to join a platoon and go out to the field. However, we didn't get many enlisted college graduates in the infantry, so I assigned him to the First Sergeant to help out with all of the reporting and record keeping that had to be done. He had everything under control in about three weeks. I never got another admin gig from the Battalion Commander or the Sergeant Major once he got in there. He was a Godsend. He let me concentrate on managing our part of the war instead of checking paperwork. Where is he now?," Marco asked.

"He's in Grand Rapids where he was from originally. He's a pretty big deal in Amway which is headquartered there. Anyhow, he's kept in touch with Golinski's family. There were three of them from Michigan that were pretty close in Vietnam Emory, Golinski and Callahan. Callahan was KIA about a month prior to Golinski's death."

"Yeah, I remember Callahan also. He was the medic that ran out in an open area to try to save another wounded soldier," Marco said softly.

"That's right. Emory used to visit his family also until they moved away. He still visits Golinski's family a few times a year. On one of his last visits, the parents expressed a strong hope that they could one day speak to people who were with Paul Golinski when he was killed."

"How are they holding up?" Marco asked with some trepidation.

"Emory says the mom still washes Paul's clothes every week. The dad is a foreman at GM and a World War II vet."

Marco's heart sunk. It was a moment before he was able to ask," Do they have any other children?"

"Paul was the only son. They have a daughter who lives in Oregon. I called them two weeks ago and told them when we would be here," he said before Marco asked the question.

Marco looked out the window of the cab feeling his apprehension of the upcoming visit intensify. Neither man said another word until the vehicle pulled up in front of the Golinski house. It was a small, modest home on a street with many similar houses. Even in January, Marco could tell that the small lawns and exteriors of the houses were neat and well cared for. He hesitated for a moment before he made an effort to leave the cab. Sergeant Cole was already outside paying the driver. He finally roused himself and exited the vehicle. He stood on the curb studying the house as the cab pulled away. He tried to imagine the laughter and love that had taken place in this house while Paul was growing up. Without going in, Marco thought he could feel the sadness and emptiness that inhabited the house now.

Sergeant Cole looked at him for a moment and then bounded up the steps. He hesitated at the door while he waited for Marco to join him on the landing. When they were together, Sergeant Cole rang the bell.

A tall, slim, graying man opened the door. Marco could see the resemblance immediately between this man and Paul Golinski. The image of the young soldier's face right before he was killed flashed across his mind. He took an involuntary step backward before he regained control of himself.

"Mr. Golinski, hi. I'm First Sergeant Cole and this is Capt. Covello. Thanks for allowing us to visit you today."

"Oh, my wife and I are so happy you were able to come. Thank you for visiting us."

Marco stepped forward and shook the extended hand of the man. It was then that he noticed an elderly woman standing behind her husband nervously wiping her hands on her apron." This is my wife Mary," he said as he stepped aside and opened the door wider."Please come in."

The small room they entered was obviously the living room. It took Marco a minute for his eyes to adjust to the dim interior of the house. The man motioned to Marco and Sergeant Cole to sit on the sofa while he and his wife sat in two heavy chairs facing them. The woman looked closely at them while unconsciously wiping her hands on her apron.

"Mr. Golinski…" Sergeant Cole began before he was interrupted.

"Please call me Paul," the man said softly. "And please call my wife Mary. We're both very grateful that you would travel such long distances to visit with us today. Dave Emory, who has been very kind to us probably told you that for many years we have been anxious to talk to anyone who was with Paul," he paused and looked down at his hands before continuing. "We were anxious to speak to anyone who was with Paul when he died. I know it will be hard for you to recall those awful days, but it will be very helpful to Mary and me to learn as much as we can about Paul's last moments. He sat back in his chair as if he was exhausted by stating his wish. His wife also sat back, dabbing tears in her eyes.

"Mr. Golinski… I'm sorry-Paul," Marco moved to the front of the sofa and spoke for the first time. The evident grief, but also the quiet strength and determination of this suffering couple to learn about how their son died gave Marco the strength he needed to overcome his own emotions. "Paul and Mary," he continued,"Sergeant Cole and I both were with young Paul when he was killed." Marco and Sergeant Cole then both painstakingly recounted every fact they could recall from that awful day 25 years earlier. The Golinskis, mainly Paul senior, asked many questions about the events that took place before, during, and after his son was killed. No fact was unimportant to him. He wanted to know what the terrain was like, what time of day it was, and what the weather was like. Mary asked only a few questions, mainly about young Paul's friends that he had mentioned in his letters.

After about a half hour there were no more questions. The room grew silent for a moment before Mary stood up and said," You must be hungry after your long trip. I have some coffee and pastries in the kitchen that I'll bring out."

"Ma'am we really can't… Marco started to say before Sergeant Cole interrupted him.

"That would be real nice of you Mary. The airlines don't give you much to eat these days so that might be the only food we get for a while."

After his wife left the room, Paul said, "Paul Jr.'s loss was especially difficult for Mary. She lost an older brother in Korea." He then retrieved a scrapbook from the table next to his chair. He opened it and removed a picture which he passed to Marco."This is Paul at his first communion."

Marco studied the photo of a smiling young boy. It was clearly a picture of the young Paul Golinski that he remembered. The eyes and the smile seem to say again to Marco,"I trust you and I know things will be okay." When he looked up, he saw Paul senior studying him." You know Paul when I told you how your son was killed, I left out one very important point. I didn't leave it out to be deceptive, I did it because it's so painful for me to recall. Your son trusted me and I coaxed him into trying to cross an open area between us because I needed the radio he was carrying." Marco was sweating now even though the house was cool.

Paul looked at him a moment before he said," I knew that." Without explaining further he withdrew several letters from the scrapbook. He opened one and began to read."Pop you remember I told you about a month ago that we got a new company commander. His name is Captain Covello. Even though he's Italian and you're Polish he reminds me a lot of you. He has that unflappable quiet strength like you do. No problem seems too big for him. He just goes around fixing things that seem to stymie other people. Kind of like when you got the car repaired and got my ticket dropped when I slid on the ice and hit the light pole. Ha-ha." Paul looked up and smiled at Marco before he continued." Captain Covello has that same insight into people that you have Pop. He's constantly moving around the company joking and bolstering the morale of the men. He greets and spends a considerable amount of time with each new replacement, something our former CO never did.

"And here's the best news. He picked me to be his RTO and promoted me to Spec Four on the spot. Now I'll get to stay close to the old man, that's what we call the CO. A lot of times he just tells me to call so-and-so and in effect I am issuing orders in his name. He could've picked anyone in the company for the job and he picked me. It's quite an honor." Paul looked up from the letter and looked at Marco and Sergeant Cole.

"He was a good soldier Paul," Sergeant Cole said.

"He was the best RTO I ever had," Marco said, his voice cracking.

"I want to read something else to you." Paul took a letter out of the second envelope. He searched the page for a moment before he found the passage he was looking for. He began to read slowly,"I don't know why men choose to put the lives of others above their own lives, but I'm grateful to have known and served with such men. Your son was one of the finest and bravest young men in my company. I will miss him greatly" Paul paused and then stared at Marco." Do you know who wrote that?" He asked finally.

Marco looked down at his clenched hands."I… I wrote that." He wanted to say more, but he was too emotional.

"That's right captain, that was in the letter you sent us right after Paul was killed. I have one more letter from Paul I'd like to read to you.""Dear Pop, sad news. Remember I told you about another boy from Detroit, Danny Callahan. Well, he was killed yesterday. He was a medic and he rushed out to treat a wounded soldier and was killed. He was a great guy. I've thought a lot about Danny and how heroic he was. I don't know what causes a man to put others lives ahead of his own, but I'm grateful that I knew and served with Danny and the others in this company like him. I hope if ever I'm challenged like Danny, I'll be as brave as he was."

Paul folded the letter tenderly and returned it to the envelope."We received that letter the day after we learned that Paul had been killed. Your letter came a week later."

When Marco looked up there were tears in his eyes."Thank you Paul," he said softly.

Just then Mary returned to the room carrying a tray with cookies and pastries. She returned to the kitchen and emerged with another tray with a coffee pot and cups.

"Finally some refreshments," Paul said cheerfully, breaking the somber mood.

As the men sipped the coffee and munched on the pastries, Sergeant Cole spoke." Dave Emory tells me you were in World War II. Paul can you tell us a little of what that was like?"

"Not much to tell," Paul answered"I landed in Normandy on D+4 and walked from France into Germany carrying a BAR."

"Certainly not much of a story there," Sergeant Cole laughed. "Only 11 months of fighting the best army in the world. And, you guys were in for the duration. You could have been in for years if the Germans hadn't surrendered and we didn't drop the bomb. We only had to do 12 months."

"Yeah, it was a difficult war. Those Germans were as tough as nails. And trying to fight and survive in that brutal Northern European winter was no picnic. However, in some ways your war was worse, mainly the hostility you had to deal with when you came home." He took a sip of coffee and then continued."We had the full support of the population back home. Almost every window on this street had a blue star or gold star in it. And when we came home, there were parades and a genuine gratitude for what we had done. Quite a bit different from your homecoming."

"It is what it is. Most of my buddies are past that now. We're content to know that we did a tough job under difficult conditions. Someday I'm convinced the country will understand the sacrifices we made. Right now emotions over the war are still a little too high. However those emotions are already starting to subside. As a matter fact, all of the unrest on college campuses ended as soon as Nixon ended the draft. It kind of makes one cynical about the true motivation of all those student protests," Sergeant Cole said with a sly laugh.

When the visit was over Marco and Sergeant Cole stood up. Marco went over to Mary and hugged her. She looked up at him and said, "It comforts me so much to know that Paul was with such caring and compassionate men as both of you when... at the end."

He then walked over to Paul Senior. "When I came here I was hoping to help both of you in some small way. Instead you both have helped me more than you'll ever know."

* * * *

Marco stood up and looked at his friends arrayed around the room. "I'd like to propose a toast. They all rose. "I propose a toast to all the Golinskis and Callahans and to all the other wonderful soldiers we were privileged to lead. They were the true heroes of our time. When their country called they responded and did not shirk their duty. They were truly like the Man in the Arena so eloquently described by Teddy Roosevelt when he said, 'It is not the critic who counts; not the man who points out how the strong man stumbles, or where the doer of deeds could have done them better. The credit belongs to the man who is actually in the arena, whose face is marred by dust and sweat and blood; who strives valiantly; who errs, who comes short again and again, because there is no effort without error and shortcoming; but who does actually strive to do the deeds; who knows great enthusiasms, the great devotions; who spends himself in a worthy cause; who at the best knows in the end the triumph of high achievement, and who at the worst, if he fails, at least fails while daring greatly, so that his place shall never be with those cold and timid souls who neither know victory nor defeat. ' They all raised their glasses and bottles and shouted, "Here, here."

After they had all taken a drink, Marco continued. "I'd also like to propose that we also toast the families of the Golinskis and the Callahans and the families of all of the other fine soldiers we served with. It is they that have continued to give us their sons and daughters throughout the history of our great country whenever they are called upon to do so. They do it with heavy hearts, but also with a continuing sense of patriotism and understanding about the need for the sacrifices that are required to maintain our Republic."

His toast was met with a loud chorus of "To the families."

And finally, a toast to us. "We did the best we could with the war they asked us to fight." With that, the men crowded around Marco and hugged one another.

CHAPTER TWENTY-ONE

WELCOME HOME

"Marco, you are one lucky dude. First you become the local hero by knocking off the guy everyone loves to hate. And now you're getting married to one of the sweetest and most attractive ladies in this town. You're not that good. Fortunately, you have me for an agent to arrange all of these things for you," Tony said with a grin.

"I know you're joking Tony, but while we're alone I want to have one serious moment, if that's possible with you," Marco grabbed Tony's arm and moved him to a corner of the room.

"You're not going to get sentimental on me are you pal?" Tony asked warily.

"Nope! I just thought since I'm about ready to get a new roommate, I ought to settle up with the old one. You and I have been together a long time and whether either of us wants to admit it or not, today marks a change. We've shared so much together, both good and bad, that even though we're different on the outside, we've grown the same on the inside. I know I don't have to tell you what's in my heart because you know it," Marco said seriously.

"You're a hell of a guy Marco, and you deserve all the best. I'm glad to have shared so much with you. I only wish more of the guys who shared the hard times could be with us today to share these good times," Tony answered." Uh-oh, now your flower is crooked. Let me fix it for you in case there are any society reporters covering this extravaganza. I'd hate for you to appear in the New York Times with a crooked flower."

"Tony, Marco, let's go. Father Panella says it's time to go," Tommy yelled into the room.

"Marco, there are no other doors out of here. It looks like we'll have to go out there," Tony said as he pushed Marco to the door.

Both men walked through a passageway where they joined the other men of the wedding party." "Okay, let's line up," Tony ordered." Wedding party, attention! Right face." The men lined up and turned right with military precision.

"Forward march." The men moved in unison out the door and into the church. As they entered the church smiling, the men took their places in front of the altar. They stood self-consciously for several moments, joking and whispering comments to each other. As the organist began the bridal march, they turned solemnly and faced the rear of the church. Marco could see Kathy smiling in the back of the church as the bridesmaids started down the aisle. Kathy and her father made their way slowly down the aisle. In contrast to Marco's nervousness, she seemed at ease as she nodded and greeted the guests on both sides of the aisle. When she got to where her mother was seated she stopped, leaned into the aisle and gently pulled her mother up.

Kathy's mother was initially surprised by this unexpected gesture. She responded warmly by hugging her daughter." I love you mom," Kathy whispered to her as they embraced. Kathy's father stood by smiling, his eyes moistened. They then resumed the march up the aisle to join Marco.

Kathy joined Marco who was now grinning broadly and the ceremony proceeded. At the end of the ceremony, Kathy and Marco still facing the altar, prepared for the recessional. The organ music began while they were still chatting with the priest. The moment Kathy heard the singer, she swiftly turned to face the choir loft. She knew immediately it was her uncle Angelo. When she saw him, she threw him a kiss. Beaming, she turned back to Marco and hugged him excitedly and then hugged Father Panella. She then walked over and hugged Tony, figuring correctly that he had helped in arranging this surprise.

Then she and Marco led the procession down the aisle to the beautiful music sung by Kathy's uncle. Kathy was even more engaging on her trip back down the aisle, waving and making comments to many of the guests. Marco feeling more confident now with Kathy by his side, smiled and nodded to those people he knew.

As the rest of the wedding party joined them, Kathy and Marco formed a receiving line at the rear of the church." Where's Tony?" Marco asked as they were greeting the guests.

"He had to do something. He said he'd be right back," Kathy said smiling.

"I hope he's not arranging a hockey game or a boxing match for me," Marco quipped.

After most of the guests passed through the receiving line and had moved outside to wait, Tony returned.

"Great Tony! You missed the receiving line. Where were you? I'm docking your best man pay 20 minutes," Marco said with a grin.

"Kathy, Marco come outside. I have another surprise for you," Tony said as he pulled them toward the door of the church. Smiling, Kathy and Marco moved toward the open church door where the wedding guests waited.

As Marco reached the door and looked outside, he recoiled as if he had seen a ghost. However, with Kathy on one arm and Tony guiding his other arm, he found himself on the landing outside the church.

On the sidewalk area below him, the men of his company had formed an honor guard in the center of all the other guests. One had his old company guidon raised while several others used canes or crutches to form an archway.

Kathy started to move toward the group. However, Marco would not move. Kathy gently released his arm and walked down the steps. As she stood amongst his company members, she held out her hand to Marco, beckoning him to join her.

Marco seemed almost to panic. Kathy ascended one step and again reached for him. This time, he slowly reached out and grabbed her hand. She then gently pulled him toward her and his waiting comrades. As she did so, they all closed in on both Kathy and Marco, hugging them and each other. Marco embraced each one of them in turn. When he turned back to Kathy, she saw a single tear roll down his cheek. She gently brushed it away with her thumb and whispered in his ear. "Welcome home Marco." He looked at her silently for a moment then buried his head in her shoulder and cried uncontrollably.

THE END